AF409911

ISBN 978-88-8398-088-6
Copyright © 2022 by European Press Academic Publishing
Florence, Italy
www.e-p-a-p.com
www.europeanpress.eu
Proprietà letteraria riservata—Printed in Italy, UK and USA

Being Europeans
in Times of Covid

Giancarlo Vilella

EUROPEAN PRESS ACADEMIC PUBLISHING

Florence, Italy

On the cover: Image from Pixabay

Articles for CERIDAP 2020-21
Preface by Prof. Diana-Urania Galetta
Coordinator of CERIDAP
and Director of the Ceridap-Journal

I would like to thank my colleague and friend Robert Bray, who has been instrumental in helping me to make my English worthy of its subject-matter: the responsibility for the remaining errors and infelicities is mine and mine alone. Although I am now retired, I would add that the views expressed in this book are my own and cannot be imputed to any institution of the Union.

Preface

by Prof. Diana-Urania Galetta

Coordinator of CERIDAP and Director of Ceridap-Journal[1]

After a long and complex gestation, the Interdisciplinary Research Centre on the Law of Public Administrations (Centro di Ricerca Interdisciplinare sul Diritto delle Amministrazioni Pubbliche – CERIDAP) was born as a Research Centre of the University of Milan (Università degli Studi di Milano) at the beginning of 2020, shortly before the Covid-19 pandemic broke out tragically in Europe, too, with its first epicentre precisely in the north of Italy.

As it happens with any new-born, the "social conditions" during its first months of life have had a profound influence on its "character" and inclinations, affecting to some extent the "genetic code" itself of CERIDAP: born with the mission of exploring, keeping track of and trying to explain the most recent evolutions in the context of Public Law and especially of the Public Administrations (the plural is necessary!), CERIDAP had to face the earthquake caused by the Covid-19 pandemic, which almost immediately had a major impact on all sectors, including (and somehow especially) the Public Administration.

In this complex and challenging context, the idea of starting

---

[1] https://ceridap.eu

to put pen to paper, in order to keep track of our reflections and debate, was a natural consequence. CERIDAP Journal was therefore born from my initiative (in my capacity as Director of the Interdisciplinary Research Centre on Public Administration), but it was a consequence of the engagement and support of a group of both enthusiastic and visionary scholars, coming from various Italian and foreign universities and who are now part of its Editorial Board. To be able to write down (and take trace of) what we were observing as to the functioning of Public Law and Public Institutions in face of such an epochal crisis was our challenge. The founding idea was to try and evaluate (and "judge of", as well) the impact of the Covid-19 pandemic on the Public Law institutions and principles we were accustomed to. The basic question was (and still is!) around the possible resilience of the Rule of Law and the institutions which have been created in order to protect it, both at the national and at the EU and International level.

From this point of view, the Covid-19 pandemic offered us a privileged observation point and a unique challenge. Nonetheless, CERIDAP was and is not just about this; and the authors of articles and comments for its journal have not devoted themselves exclusively to this matter.

The aim of the CERIDAP Journal is, in fact, to provide a contribution of analysis, in-depth review and proposals with the main focus being Public Administrations: seen from their institutional, organizational and activity dimensions, as well as from their procedural dimension. Such analysis takes into account a natural opening also to a Comparative, European and International Law perspective, as well as an opening to interdisciplinary discussion, which is supported by the presence of prominent scholars in its Scientific Committee from prestigious universities around the world.

Giancarlo Vilella – at the time still Director General of the DG for Innovation and Technological Support of the European

Parliament (DG ITEC) – has been part of CERIDAP Research Centre from the very beginning and is a member of its (very small) Steering Committee. He was an enthusiastic supporter (and part of) all efforts we had to make in order to make CERIDAP Research Centre and CERIDAP Journal take their first steps in what we hope is the right direction. He has generously made available his experience and expertise as high-profile Civil Servant, who has authored (in over forty years of intense activity as a scholar and publicist) several books and essays on Public Administration and on the European Union, including four highly appreciated articles for CERIDAP Journal, which are somehow the perfect "children" of our complex time: as they focus on the two highly intertwined topics of the consequences of the Covid-19 emergency and the role of the European Union.

Those four articles are now put together in this book and republished, together with a final chapter devoted to some "Conclusions" and which aims at recapitulating the route traced by the four articles written for CERIDAP.

The evolution of Public Administrations constantly moves from the legal, regulatory and jurisprudential perspective, which informs every organization and activity. Public Administrations, to extricate themselves from a complex and multidimensional administrative system, must necessarily integrate broad and diverse knowledge, and specific and interdisciplinary expertise. If CERIDAP is therefore a "place" for in-depth study and research on issues related to the functioning of the Public Administration, which needs to take into account both the purely legal aspects and those related to political science in order to understand the needs of society and the social sphere, the interdisciplinary skills of its members and collaborators are a *conditio sine qua non* for being able to do its job properly.

Giancarlo Vilella, with his reflections which are the result of a vast and wide-reaching experience both as a high-level Civil Servant and as a Public-Science scholar, has given an essential contribution to the birth and growth of CERIDAP, both as a Research Centre and as a Journal: this book is a concrete evidence of that. I can therefore only hope that he is willing to go on doing so for a long, long time!

Milan, 13th October 2021

Table of Contents

Introduction

The creation and impetus of the Interdisciplinary Research Centre on Public Administration (CERIDAP) at the University of Milan, under the brilliant leadership of Professor Diana-Urania Galetta[2], came at the very moment when the Covid emergency burst on to the scene. It was plain from the outset that the pandemic would have a major impact on all sectors, including institutions and the administration, but already today (without waiting for the time when history will judge) we can say that it had an epochal impact, in the sense that it made us reflect seriously about the resilience of the "systems" (political, legal, health, economic, educational, etc.) and their prospects. Fortunately, the scholars who refer to CERIDAP and the authors of essays for its journal have not devoted themselves exclusively to this matter, but a good deal of their reflections have been influenced by it. This influence was certainly true of my own contribution, which took the form of four articles on topics firmly laced together by two closely interwoven threads: the consequences of the Covid emergency and the role of the European Union. This homogeneous character of the four articles persuaded me (and prompted many to encourage me) to bring them together in this volume as a single reflection, rounded off by some final (unpublished) considerations on the way ahead.

---

[2]Whom I thank most sincerely for the Preface with which she lends lustre to this book.

Chapter 1

Parliamentary democracy facing Coronavirus by (also) technologies

Rivista Interdisciplinare sul Diritto delle Amministrazioni Pubbliche

Fascicolo 1/2020

Gennaio – Marzo

Abstract (Italian): [La democrazia parlamentare di fronte al Coronavirus mediante (anche) le tecnologie] *L'emergenza sanitaria Covid-19 ha fra i tanti effetti anche quello di mettere sotto pressione le istituzioni democratiche nel loro funzionamento: in particolare i parlamenti sono costretti a cedere spazio agli esecutivi a causa della situazione eccezionale. Se non si prendono le giuste misure a questo proposito, ci sono certamente rischi per la democrazia nel prossimo futuro. L'articolo esamina i vari dettagli dell'operazione, sia dal punto di vista delle regole che dal punto di vista delle soluzioni tecnologiche. Si tratta di un'esperienza rilevante per gli sviluppi futuri.*

Among its many effects, the Covid-19 health emergency has put the functioning of democratic institutions under an unusual pressure. Parliaments are forced to give the executive branch powers to deal with the exceptional situation the virus has created. If proper balancing measures are not taken, there are risks for democracy in the near future. The article examines how the EU Parliament has faced this challenge, both from a legal point of view, and the technological solutions that have been implemented. The aim is to provide a relevant example for future developments.

When the Coronavirus Covid-19 emergency broke out, the search for solutions for the proper functioning of the parliamentary institutions required reflection (*inter alia*) on the use of technologies in such situations. The Covid-19 emergency has even brought many analysts to the conclusion that the situation is a risk for democracy: for instance, the successful author Y. N. Harari says that "the storm will pass, humankind will survive, most of us will still be alive – but we will inhabit a different world[1]". What world? It depends on the choices we make: "The first" – says Harari – "is between totalitarian surveillance and citizen empowerment"[2]. He is not alone in taking this view. Another example, among many, is the appeal made to the institutions by a group of intellectuals in Italy[3]: the appeal contends that "all at home" (confinement) is poisonous for the institutions because it puts democracy into quarantine. According to the authors of the appeal, Parliament assembles only intermittently, converts decrees into laws hastily and does not exercise its power of holding the executive to account; the government meets at night and communicates through social media; the Prime Minister limits

---

[1]Y.N. HARARI, *The world after coronavirus*, Financial Times, 20 March 2020.

[2]ibid.

[3]The first signatory was Prof. Marcello Pera, a former President of the Senate of the Italian Republic: see Corriere della Sera, 25 March 2020.

constitutional rights by decree, and so on. Democracy cannot be suspended, the appeal says, because if "you resign yourself to something today, you will lose freedom tomorrow". The question has also been raised in Belgium, to mention another example, on account of the exceptional powers (*"pouvoirs spéciaux"*) conferred on federal or regional executives: here too, the question is whether the guarantees of democratic control are ensured and remain sufficient if parliament (with the regional parliaments) continues to exercise its activities but with means and methods adapted to the situation[4]. In short, also an emergency (in this case a health emergency, but we have also experienced a terrorist emergency) is a factor which puts parliamentary democracy at risk. So, what is the situation? A clear and dynamic picture is offered by the Inter-Parliamentary Union (IPU) based in Geneva. In an *ad hoc* permanently updated document[5] we can read the following:

- *"A short survey circulated by the ECPRD suggests that most European Parliaments continue to operate but in a limited manner. Most restrictions are to limit unnecessary access to buildings, for staff and members to work remotely where they can. The majority of parliaments continue to sit albeit in more limited ways and, in a number of cases, with fewer members being present (issues of ensuring parliament is quorate arise in some cases). Some parliaments have taken an early recess or changed their operating procedures so that a special committee sits, rather than the whole house.*

- *Significant numbers of staff are now working remotely. This presents challenges in terms of maintaining operational systems. Though some of these can be supported remotely,*

---

[4]See in particular the extensive inquiry of Bernard Demonty in Le Soir of 26 March 2020.

[5]IPU-Centre for Innovation in Parliament, *Parliamentary Responses to Coronavirus*, Live Document, March 2020.

> *this is designed for exceptions rather than the norm when a parliament is sitting. There will increasingly be issues with unavailability of staff and third-party support due to illness".*

The European Parliament has also adopted solutions for the proper functioning of the institution and this in turn meant that we had to reflect on the use of technology in such situations. To a large extent, what we have been looking at is the possibility of effective remote working of MEPs and staff. In this sense, in the midst of the emergency created by the spread of Covid-19, DG ITEC[6] sent an internal note to all staff, entitled "Teleworking facilities", which listed the available possibilities: connecting from your personal laptop; token access for security; email access through webmail; extranet access; jabber access; VDI for remote access; email access on phone or tablet; hybrids. By recalling what the "normal" tools available are, the note implicitly underscores their usefulness in times of emergency. The services then got to work to strengthen these capabilities.

An important decision of the President of the European Parliament, David Sassoli, has paved the way for reflection on a more advanced experiment with digitisation in the exercise of democratic functions: what I mean is an experiment not limited only to supporting the functioning of the institution, but where we get to exercise the powers of the democratic system through digitisation. This would be a significant development. We read in the preamble to President Sassoli's decision[7], "while protecting health, Parliament as a critical infrastructure of democracy in the European Union should retain its capacity to exercise its core functions as attributed to the Institution by the Treaty on European Union; information technology tools should, to the extent possible, replace physical meetings and thus contribute to

---

[6]That is the ICT Department of the European Parliament.

[7]Decision of the President of the European Parliament, CP D(2020)9886, Brussels, 9 March 2020.

enabling Parliament to exercise its core functions" and, in the operative part, "the Secretary-General shall take the measures necessary to enable remote participation to meetings of Parliament's governing bodies, committees and the plenary, without prejudice to decisions of the Bureau of the European Parliament on matters relating to the conduct of sittings." The implementation of these instructions will involve the provision of advanced IT tools, which is certainly essential if the operation is to be a success. The implementation of the Presidents requests has been immediate and effective. In a Note of the Secretary General the following 18 March[8] we can read that: "With the view to ensuring the continuity of the Members' exercise of their duties related to parliamentary activity, the services of the European Parliament's administration have been asked to implement measures to facilitate the remote participation of Members in parliamentary activities in the current prolonged situation of Force Majeure where they cannot physically attend the meetings. Remote participation means being able to view and listen to proceedings, ask for the floor and intervene in the meeting. (...) Four meeting rooms have been equipped to be operational to host parliamentary meetings (...) With this solution, both the Members participating directly from the Parliament's meeting room and those participating remotely will be able to express themselves (...) The tool also offers the possibility of remote polling. Whether this feature is used or not is a political decision." That's what can be called a frank successful reaction from the administration point of view, in such an emergency conditions.

It is clear that its development towards something that we can call digital democracy will depend exclusively on the rules determining how we are to operate in the new way: these rules will be a fundamental and founding element of any digital democracy. They are the essential precursor and indeed a *sine qua*

---

[8]Der Generalsekretär, *Remote participation for Members in Parliamentary activities,* D(2020)10901, 18 March 2020.

non for the launch of any form of digital democracy. In the specific circumstance of the Covid-19 emergency, the need for specific rules for a digital vote was very clear to top management, both administrative and political, and so urgent ad hoc measures were taken. An extraordinary meeting of the Bureau was convened to adopt rules derogating from the Rules of Procedure on the basis of a proposal submitted by the Secretary General. This action was manifestly necessary and urgent in order for Parliament to adopt Commission proposals (under the ordinary legislative procedure) which were of an urgent nature and designed to deploy common European actions to counter the problems arising from Covid-19: Parliament was convened to meet in plenary session on 26 March 2020 with the aim of adopting the European Commission's proposals. The preparatory file for the Bureau meeting[9] describes precisely why, how and when it was intended to proceed so as to allow MEPs to vote remotely:

"In light of the current situation and the overriding public health restrictions on, inter alia, travel applicable to some Members, as well as the need for Parliament to be in a position to adopt the urgent measures proposed by the Commission as part of the EU-coordinated response to COVID-19, it is proposed that the Bureau supplement its 2004 Decision on rules governing voting.

The proposal in the annex to the note from the Secretary-General seeks to allow for a temporary derogation on public health grounds, upon decision by the President, to enable the vote to take place by an alternative electronic voting procedure, with adequate safeguards to ensure that Members' votes are individual, personal and free, in line with the provisions of the Electoral act and the Members' Statute.

In particular, Members would receive electronically, via email

---

[9]TECHNICAL NOTES for the extraordinary meeting of the BUREAU on Friday 20 March 2020, Brussels, PE 649.203/BUR.

to their official email address, a ballot form, which would be returned, completed, from their email address to the relevant Parliament's functional mailbox. The results of all votes conducted under this temporary derogation would be recorded in the minutes of the sitting concerned. This decision would remain in force until its repeal by the Bureau, once the public health emergency has abated".

The Bureau confirmed and adopted the proposal, by attributing to the President the full power to decide "if and when" to use the alternative method of voting[10]. The technical solution adopted was as simple as effective, that's the following: *Where the President has decided under Article 1 that the alternative electronic voting system shall be used, the voting shall take place in accordance with the following arrangements:*

1. *The voting list as well as the opening time and closing time of the vote shall be published on Parliament's website. The voting list, the ballot form as well as the opening time and closing time of the vote shall be sent by electronic mail from the mailbox "plenaryvote@europarl.europa.eu" to the professional mailbox of each Member.*

2. *The Member shall vote by filling in and signing the ballot form on paper.*

3. *The Member shall send a copy of his or her ballot form, scanned or photographed in PDF, JPG or any similar standard electronic format allowing for a clear and readable image, by electronic mail from his or her professional mailbox to the mailbox "plenaryvote@europarl.europa.eu".*

4. *The President shall establish the result of the vote on the basis of the ballot forms which comply with the requirements of points (b) and (c) and have been received before or at the closing time mentioned in point (a).*

---

[10]DECISION OF THE BUREAU OF THE EUROPEAN PARLIAMENT of 20 March 2020 supplementing its Decision of 3 May 2004 on rules governing voting, PE 649.211/BUR

> 5. *The use of the alternative electronic voting system shall be recorded in the minutes of the sitting, together with the result of the vote*[11].

The two intelligent ideas underlying this proposal are, firstly, maximum simplification of the voting mechanism (exchange of e-mails), which avoids the technical and legal problems associated with online voting, and, secondly, the temporary and exceptional nature of the action, precisely because its simplicity can only be a one-off.

As I said earlier, in fact, if you want to insert online remote voting into a "normal" mechanism for the functioning of democratic powers, the rules must be deepened and detailed. The EP, in this case, needs to revise or to complete the following body of regulations. Rule 186 of the Rules of Procedure, on the right to vote, which provides that the right to vote is a personal right and Members shall cast their votes individually and in person. Rule 187 of the Rules of Procedure, on voting, which empowers the President to decide at any time that the voting operations be carried out by means of an electronic voting system. Rule 192 of the Rules of Procedure, on the use of the electronic voting system which provides, in paragraph 1, that the Bureau shall lay down instructions determining the technical arrangements for use of the electronic voting system. The Bureau Decision of 3 May 2004 on rules governing voting, as amended, which lays down the technical arrangements for electronic voting. Of course, it must be clear, you need the rules are underpinned by a much more complex technological support than a mere e-mail.

However, the experience gained as a result of Covid-19 is a very useful and important starting point, should ever the European Parliament wish to move towards a systematic solution. And possibly, it could be reference for other Parliaments.

---

[11]*Ibid.* art. 2.

Chapter 2

Managing in times of crisis: the case of the European Parliament

Rivista Interdisciplinare sul Diritto delle Amministrazioni Pubbliche

Fascicolo 1/2021

Gennaio – Marzo

Abstract (Italian): *I punti essenziali del ragionamento sviluppato in questo articolo sono: il Covid-19 ha messo in evidenza il ruolo svolto dall'amministrazione come ponte nel confronto (conflittuale) tra il potere della scienza e il potere politico; l'emergenza sanitaria ha messo in luce l'importanza del funzionamento delle istituzioni parlamentari per la difesa della democrazia dato che il potere esecutivo (oggettivamente) ha il sopravvento. L'amministrazione del Parlamento europeo è un caso di studio molto interessante in questo senso perché è riuscita a far fronte all'emergenza grazie a diversi fattori; l'EPA ha attuato negli ultimi anni un programma di digitalizzazione strutturale del Parlamento europeo. Infine, l'EPA ha lavorato per attivare una capacità amministrativa per gestire le "misure senza precedenti" che si sono dovute adottare: tale capacità è stata raggiunta realizzando le azioni nel rigoroso quadro della governance del Parlamento europeo e sotto il suo controllo permanente.*

The essential points of the reasoning developed in this article are: Covid-19 has brought to the fore the role played by the administration as a bridge in the (conflictual) confrontation between the power of science and political power; the health emergency has cast light on the importance of the functioning of parliamentary institutions for the defence of democracy because the executive branch (objectively) gets the upper hand. The administration of the European Parliament is a very interesting case study in this respect because it has succeeded in coping with the emergency thanks to several factors; EPA implemented a programme of structural digitisation of the European Parliament in recent years. Finally, EPA worked for activating an administrative capacity to manage the "unprecedented measures" that had to be adopted: this capacity was achieved by carrying out the actions within the strict framework of the governance of the European Parliament and under its permanent scrutiny.

The emergency caused by the Covid-19 pandemic has cast light on the important role played by the public administration in managing the crisis, and in particular the central role of its management. Recently, Zeger Van der Wal explained in a very pertinent way[1] that the capacity of the public administration is an essential factor for ensuring resilience, trust and an exit from the crisis: in this context, the public managers are those who work behind the scenes, in a complex and uncertain environment, to deliver results. Van der Wal identifies three "key competences" which managers must know how to use for smart management in times of crisis, such as that of Covid-19: explaining and selling unprecedented measures; astute relationship with the political masters; empowering and leveraging networks. This is an interesting suggestion, following which I would put

---

[1]Zeger VAN DER WAL, Being a Public Manager in Times of Crisis: The Art of Managing Stakeholders, Political Masters, and Collaborative Networks, in Public Administration Review, Vol. 80, Iss. 5, 2020, pp. 759-764.

forward some considerations on the experience of the European Parliament as a case study.

First, however, I must add that in a situation such as the health emergency that we are currently undergoing, the role played by the administration is much more delicate than just ensuring good management, because it is intended above all to ensure balance in the ongoing conflict between powerful actors in our societies, namely science and politics. Max Weber was way ahead of his time when he identified the development of this conflict a century ago[2]. As Weber explained in a way that has never been unsurpassed, the three essential subjects/protagonists are: science/technology, the political sphere and the administration. Weber understood perfectly where we were going a century ago and his analysis is altogether suited to the current situation, specifically in the context of the Covid-19 emergency: in fact, the three protagonists in question are hard at work. Weber explains that in modern times the main dialectic, which in truth is a relationship that tends to be conflictual, is between science/technology and the political sphere: in both cases, Weber said, evolution would lead to their professionalisation, to the disenchantment of the world, risking a separation that will have to be reconciled. On the one hand, there is science/technology, concentrated on its subject-matter in complete autonomy and with its tendency to be hegemonic; on the other hand, there is the political sphere, which has to come to terms with science/technology, but must be able to take the most appropriate decisions, that is to say, must be able to decide having regard to

---

[2]I am referring, of course, to the two essays, The Vocation Lectures (Edited and with an Introduction by D. OWEN and T.B. STRONG, Translation by R. LIVINGSTONE), Hackett, Indianapolis/Cambridge, 2004: this book brings together the celebrated lectures given by Max Weber in Vienna (1917-1919) on "Wissenschaft als Beruf" and "Politik als Beruf". However, for the considerations that follow I have taken my inspiration from Massimo CACCIARI, Il lavoro dello spirito. Saggio su Max Weber, Adelphi, Milano, 2020, essay on "geistige Arbeit".

all the elements necessary for the government of society and not only the subject-matter of science. This is exactly what we are experiencing today in general terms with technological progress, which tends to be hegemonic and separated from the political sphere, while the latter tries to bring everything back together within the framework of a global governance of society: and this has been accentuated by Covid-19. The question is: where is the factor of possible reconciliation to be found? The philosopher Massimo Cacciari, reconstructing Weber's thought, tells us: *«Without a technical-bureaucratic apparatus, without organisation, without skills, politics is not a profession, and will therefore necessarily be ineffective in governing a world dominated by technical/scientific powers. A political sphere which does not want or is unable to structure itself professionally internally and equip itself as a whole with powerful administrative/bureaucratic structures will simply be opting for impotence».*[3]

Generally, when we speak of the public administration, we mean administration acting at the level of government, the executive branch, and we also include local and regional authorities, always as executive branch. Van der Wal is no exception and focuses on this type of administration and management. Well, this is a very serious limitation in scholarly literature in general, but it becomes really serious problem when it comes to emergency situations of the type brought about by Covid-19. The reason is very clear: Y. N. Harari says that *«the storm will pass, humankind will survive, most of us will still be alive – but we will inhabit a different world»*. What world? It depends on the choices we make: *«The first»* – says Harari – *«is between totalitarian surveillance and citizen empowerment»*[4]. He is not alone in taking this view, the debate on this issue over the past year has been very intense and wide-ranging. An example, among many,

---

[3]CACCIARI, cited in the preceding note (translated by the author).

[4]Y.N. HARARI, The world after coronavirus, Financial Times, 20 March 2020.

is the appeal made to the institutions by a group of intellectuals in Italy[5]: the appeal contends that "all at home" (confinement) is poisonous for the institutions because it puts democracy into quarantine. According to the authors of the appeal, Parliament assembles only intermittently, converts decrees into laws hastily and does not exercise its power of holding the executive to account; the government meets at night and communicates through social media; the Prime Minister limits constitutional rights by decree, and so on. Democracy cannot be suspended, the appeal says, because if *«you resign yourself to something today, you will lose freedom tomorrow».*

In short, also an emergency (in this case a health emergency, but we have experienced a terrorism emergency or immigration emergency too) is a factor which puts democracy at risk, especially its representative institutions such as parliaments: this is the reason why there is general agreement on the need to set strict time limits to special powers in emergency situations, such as that of Covid-19, in democratic countries, where, moreover, it must be obligatory to justify them, but at the same time do everything to allow parliaments to continue to function and exercise their powers.

The European Parliament was among the first (or perhaps the first) to become aware of the situation, as can be seen from the stances it adopted as early as April 2019, that is to say, a few weeks after the emergency erupted. A Resolution[6] adopted by the Plenary, the European Parliament's highest political level, clearly states: *«the Charter of Fundamental Rights of the European Union and compliance with the rule of law must continue to apply, and ... in the context of emergency measures, the au-*

---

[5]The first signatory was Prof. Marcello Pera, a former President of the Senate of the Italian Republic: see Corriere della Sera, 25 March 2020.

[6]European Parliament resolution of 17 April 2020 on EU coordinated action to combat the COVID-19 pandemic and its consequences, P9_TAPROV(2020)0054.

thorities must ensure that everyone enjoys the same rights and protection; ... all measures taken at national and/or EU level must be in line with the rule of law, strictly proportionate to the exigencies of the situation, clearly related to the ongoing health crisis, limited in time and subjected to regular scrutiny». The President of Parliament, David Maria Sassoli, himself made a statement, saying: *«Our message is clear: democracy continues to function; all parliamentary bodies are continuing to work to tackle the Covid-19 emergency. We have ensured that MEPs are still able to meet remotely, participate in debates, propose amendments and vote. Democracy will continue»*[7]. It is important to remind that the EP confirmed its approach during the whole 2020 year and obtained significant results in the adoption of the Multiannual Financial Framework 2021-2027, the Interinstitutional Agreement, the EU Recovery Instrument and the Rule of Law Regulation[8]. In the related Resolution, after having stressed that an effective Rule of Law Regulation and the introduction of new own resources were a pre-condition of the European Parliament to agree with the MFF package, the EP at par. 9 *«stresses that co-legislators have agreed that the Regulation on a general regime of conditionality for the protection of the Union budget shall apply from 1 January 2021 and will have to be applied to all commitments and payments; expects the Commission, as the guardian of the Treaties, to ensure that the Regulation is fully applicable from the date agreed by the co-legislators and recalls that annulment of the Regulation or part of it is only possible by the CJEU»* and added that the Parliament will defend its validity before the Court and expects the Commission to intervene in support of Parliament's position.

Now the question is as simple as it is frequently (or always)

---

[7]The passage in italics is taken word for word from the report in the POLITICO Brussels Playbook of 3 April 2020.

[8]European Parliament resolution of 17 December 2020, P9_TA-PROV(2020)0360.

forgotten: who makes it possible that *all parliamentary bodies can continue to work to tackle the Covid-19 emergency?* Who ensures *that MEPs are still able to meet remotely, participate in debates, propose amendments and vote?* The answer is just as simple: it is the administration of the European Parliament (EPA). The EPA case study is a success story from which the following lesson can be drawn: in order to deal successfully with an emergency situation such as Covid-19, it is not enough to activate good managerial capacities, it is necessary that the administration should already have a solid basis for action and structures already prepared to adapt to unforeseen situations. What I mean is that what is "unforeseen" must be the situation which has to be tackled, not what the administration has to do. Under the leadership of Secretary General Klaus Welle and with the support of top management, the EPA has worked steadily over the last ten years to prepare these solid foundations by following two parallel but connected paths: on the one hand, by pursuing innovation in working methods, on the other, by achieving the digitisation of the institution. It is thanks to this that the response to the Covid-19 emergency was excellent and the European Parliament has continued to function.

As far as working methods are concerned[9], the EPA has built a management system step by step, based on the method of combining vision and planning, together with the approach of a joint use of a matrix and metrics. The "vision" takes into account the context (internal and external) in which the work is performed, thanks to an analysis of what is happening and what could happen. "Planning" determines the adoption of projects coordinated

---

[9]For an in-depth, detailed analysis of this aspect, see G. VILELLA, Working methods of the European Parliament Administration in Multi-actors World. A case-study, European Press Academic Publishing, Florence, 2019: I carried out this study pursuant to a formal mandate from Secretary General K. Welle (in agreement with the then President of Parliament, A. Tajani) and developed it during a research period at the European University Institute in Florence

by sectors, with a clear indication of the objectives and responsibilities. Vision and planning together give rise to the Strategic Execution Framework, a planning document for a three-year period, which is the reference for the long-term work of the European Parliament's administration. The "matrix" approach establishes the interrelationships between the various projects and objectives, thus fostering internal cooperation, whilst the "metrics" approach allows for permanent measurement and scrutiny of the results achieved: what is interesting in the EPA's experience is that an effort is made (with difficulty, but consistently) to ensure that the two aspects (matrix/metrics) are not separated.

As far as the digitisation of the institution is concerned[10], the EPA has succeeded in making the European Parliament a parliamentary world leader in the use of technology for its activities thanks to its awareness of the importance of that process in the future: significant financial and human resources have been made available for this purpose. Over a number of years, up to the 2019 elections, the digitisation of the institution has seen the implementation of: eCommittee, eMeeting, the Drafting Support Tool, AT4AM, Digital Signature, ICT services for constituency offices, XML, metadata and indexing, eVote. As of 2019, a new programme that we find described in a DG ITEC document[11] is being implemented: it identifies the strate-

---

[10]See G. VILELLA, The European Parliament Administration facing the challenge of eDemocracy, European Press Academic Publishing, Florence, 2021, for a detailed, in- depth appraisal of this aspect: this study was also carried out on basis of a formal mandate from Secretary General K. Welle (in agreement with President D. M. Sassoli). For further particulars, see also G. VILELLA, E-Democracy. Dove ci porta la democrazia digitale, Pendragon, Bologna, 2020, in particular on the European Parliament, at pp. 233-262

[11]Information and Communication Technology (ICT) in the European Parliament: Strategic orientations 2019-2021, authored by W. Petrucci, with the agreement of the Secretary General, D(2019)34304, October 2019. This is a Note to the Members of the Bureau Working Party on ICT Innovation Strategy

gic guidelines for the current (9th) legislature, whereby the aim
is to accelerate the digital transformation of the Institution by
means of a number of projects. We find a package of projects designed to increase DG ITEC's ability to be more resilient, open
and efficient: service improvement, cybersecurity, metrics collec-
tion, contract staff, meeting customers' needs and IT capacity
building for democracy support. DG ITEC wishes to help other
parliaments become more transparent, accountable and effective through the development of IT governance and the sharing
of knowledge. Next, we find a second package of projects cal-
culated to improve the digital workplace (for MEPs, assistants
and staff): ICT support, needs-based printing, the ITEC cat-
alogue of services and Parliamentary open data. In addition,
there are two other projects, referred to as game changers: that
is to say, speeding up the move towards cloud computing and
artificial intelligence (AI). These plans are a clear contribution
to strengthening parliamentary democracy through a process of
digital transformation. In short, when the Covid-19 emergency
erupted in the first months of 2020, the EPA did not have to
invent a new type of management to deal with it, but had to be
able to adapt its solid structure – based on innovative working
methods and advanced digitisation – to the new situation. As
I said just now: to deal successfully with an emergency situation like Covid-19, it is not enough to activate good managerial
skills, it is necessary that the administration should already have
a sound basis for action. This does not mean, of course, that the
activation of good managerial skills is not equally necessary: the
three "key competences" identified by Van der Wal, in fact, are
well suited to the experience of the EPA, as is the context which
he adumbrates. It is true, as Van der Wal says, that Covid-19
requires us to act in a complex, volatile and uncertain environment, for which flexibility, unconventional expertise and strategy
are necessary: the EPA has been able to adapt to the new situation thanks (as we have seen above) to its habit which has

evolved over many years of working on a strategic plan, of imagining and developing projects, not for here and now, but for the future, and of using sophisticated technological support. These are all things that have fostered a propensity for flexibility and a willingness to learn new skills.

Even the EPA had to take "unprecedented measures" to make the institution work, mainly in the use of technology and logistics. As for the former, what we have been looking at is the possibility of effective remote working of MEPs and staff: connecting from their personal laptops; token access for security; email access through webmail; extranet access; jabber access; VDI for remote access; email access on phone or tablet; hybrids. Information technology tools had to replace physical meetings and thus contribute to enabling Parliament to exercise its core functions and to enabling remote participation in meetings of Parliament's governing bodies, committees and the plenary, including electronic voting. As for logistics, the actions taken were conceived in two stages, first the immediate and urgent reaction, then the definition of a "new" normality[12]. First, early reaction: almost immediate and complete lock-down of Parliament's premises from a logistics perspective (while fully ensuring both political and administrative activities); no physical presence allowed and a massive teleworking scheme (100% except essential services); first limited and targeted distribution of protective devices (masks, gloves, gel, plexiglas screens); only virtual meetings (both political and administrative); cancellation of missions between the three sites; re-adaptation of office space allocation observing social distancing; cancellation of public activities/no visitors allowed; stop to "on premises" services

---

[12]For the logistics aspects, I am indebted to the excellent and very clear description given by Gabriele BABINI, Logistics and Covid-19 pandemic. The European Parliament experience, PDF seminal presentation online, Brussels, 2 November 2020: the interventions I describe in the text can be found in slides 5 and 6 of this brilliant presentation.

for staff and Members (e.g. catering, transport); stop to maintenance and construction works (external contractors). Then, new normality: gradual return to the office, introduction of a 70%, 80%, 90% teleworking scheme according to the activities' criticality level; set up of a structured distribution of protective devices to staff; introduction of a temperature scan at the entrances to Parliament's premises (re-deployment of some staff, mail ushers vs print-shop staff); widespread installation of gel distributors in the institution's buildings; increased and massive distribution to staff of equipment (IT and non-IT) at home to improve ergonomics (portable devices, screens, keyboards, mice, ergonomic chairs); mixed mode meetings, both virtual and in presence; gradual reopening to visitors and public facilities with reduced availability and respecting safety measures; partial reopening of catering facilities with a reduced offer (addition of a take-away option); re-start of maintenance and construction works respecting security measures (external contractors).

Frankly, I think I can say that we have before us a clear vision of how to intervene, even if these are "unprecedented measures". The method used for explaining and selling these measures to MEPs, staff, the other institutions and external users (journalists, researchers, citizens), i.e. the EPA's stakeholders, follows a strict principle: to act exclusively within the framework of European Parliament governance. All decisions were agreed upon in advance by the Secretary General with the President before being drawn up; they were then submitted to the Bureau for confirmation (if urgent) or for decision if deferred; lastly, top management exercised permanent scrutiny of the effects of the measures taken, whilst the Secretary General presented regularly (at least once a month, or even more frequently) a detailed report on how things were proceeding. The management, therefore, acted in permanent contact with the governance of the institution, which also meets the requirements of the relationship with the political master. Finally, as regards the strengthening of collaborative works, the approach already introduced by the EPA of tuning matrixes and metrics has had the effect of bringing the various services into tune with each other in a truly exceptional manner.

To conclude[13], it is worthwhile summarising the essential points of the reasoning developed in this article. In the first place, Covid-19 has brought to the fore the role played by the administration in the Weberian sense, that is to say, as a bridge in the (conflictual) confrontation between the power of science and political power: gaining awareness of this helps to develop administrative capacities. Secondly, the health emergency we are now living through has cast light on the importance of the functioning of parliamentary institutions for the defence of democracy because the executive branch (objectively) gets the upper hand: the administrations of parliaments play a decisive role here. The administration of the European Parliament is a very interesting case study in this respect because it has succeeded in coping with the emergency thanks to several factors. The first factor is that over the last ten years the EPA has developed new working methods based on vision/planning and a matrix/metrics: this has proved a sound basis for dealing with the emergency because it has fostered the necessary planning capacity and administrative cooperation. The second factor is that the EPA implemented a programme of structural digitisation of the European Parliament in recent years: this also proved to be a winning element in dealing with the situation because the technologies were essential in order to make the machine work. The third factor consisted in activating an administrative capacity to manage the "unprecedented measures" that had to be adopted: this capacity was achieved by carrying out the actions within the strict framework of the governance of the European Parliament and under its permanent scrutiny.

---

[13]By closing this article, I wish to thank Prof. Maddalena Sorrentino, UNIMI, for the inputs she gave me in conceiving it.

Chapter 3

Lavoro e tecnologie informatiche. Note a margine della fiducia al governo Draghi

Rivista Interdisciplinare sul Diritto delle Amministrazioni Pubbliche

Fascicolo 2/2021

Aprile – Giugno

Abstract (English): *The Draghi government has taken office at a time when the labour market, characterised by the decisive influence of information technologies and a high degree of mobility, is undergoing great changes. The emergence of the pandemic, which had been underway for almost a year when the Draghi government was sworn in, has hit the labour market with the destruction of jobs and the failure to create new ones, while at the same time accentuating the disruptive processes underway (IT, mobility). The phenomenon is supranational, and the European Union is acting on two levels: facing up to the emergency (SURE, Youth initiative, EU Next Generation, etc.) and intervening on the basis of a strategy focused on investment in information technologies. It is these technologies which are changing production processes and how trades and professions are carried out, reshaping the labour market while making it necessary for workers to upskill and have IT profiles and creating a strong asymmetry between workers and their employment prospects. The Premier's speech and the government's programme are taking this problem into account: on the one hand, they have announced reforms of the assegno di riallocazione "reallocation allowance" and of job centres, on the other hand, they are talking about strengthening infrastructure (broadband, 5G) and the transversality of the Digital Transition. All of which seems appropriate. The hope is that all this will be done in the European strategic context and that the employment market becomes the omnipresent pivot of the transversal transition.*

Il governo Draghi si è insediato in un momento in cui il mercato del lavoro, caratterizzato dall'influenza decisiva delle tecnologie informatiche e da un alto grado di mobilità, sta subendo grandi cambiamenti. L'emergere della pandemia, in corso da quasi un anno al momento del giuramento del governo Draghi, ha colpito il mercato del lavoro con la distruzione di posti di lavoro e la mancata creazione di nuovi, accentuando allo stesso tempo il processo di cambiamento in corso (informatica, mobilità). Il fenomeno è sovranazionale, e l'Unione Europea sta agendo su due livelli: affrontando l'emergenza (SURE, iniziativa Giovani, EU Next Generation, ecc.) e intervenendo sulla base di una strategia incentrata sugli investimenti nelle tecnologie informatiche. Sono queste tecnologie che stanno cambiando i processi produttivi e le modalità di svolgimento dei mestieri e delle professioni, rimodellando il mercato del lavoro e rendendo necessario l'aggiornamento e il profilo informatico dei lavoratori e creando una forte asimmetria tra i lavoratori e le loro prospettive occupazionali. Il discorso del premier e il programma di governo tengono conto di questo problema: da un lato hanno annunciato riforme dell'assegno di riallocazione e dei centri per l'impiego, dall'altro parlano di rafforzamento delle infrastrutture (banda larga, 5G) e della trasversalità della transizione digitale. Tutto ciò sembra appropriato. La speranza è che tutto questo venga fatto nel contesto strategico europeo e che il mercato del lavoro diventi il perno onnipresente della transizione trasversale.

Durante l'emergenza Covid ho continuato ad analizzare il ruolo che le tecnologie, in particolare le ICT, vanno via via occupando nel mondo contemporaneo, con una particolare attenzione al funzionamento della democrazia[1]. Non v'è dubbio che l'appor-

---

[1]In particolare con la pubblicazione di G. Vilella, *eDemocracy. Dove ci porta la democrazia digitale*, Pendragon, Bologna, 2020. Successivamente con la pubblicazione di G. Vilella, *The European Parliament Administration facing the challenge of eDemocracy*, European Press Academic Publishing,

to delle tecnologie informatiche alla difesa della democrazia è stato, in questa fase di emergenza sanitaria, enormemente positivo: il funzionamento delle istituzioni parlamentari e rappresentative in genere, come anche il controllo di quello che stava succedendo da parte dei cittadini sono stati possibili grazie a queste tecnologie. Tuttavia, benché la mia attenzione fosse essenzialmente concentrata sull'aspetto della democrazia, non mi sfuggiva affatto (a me come a tanti) il ruolo egualmente importante che le tecnologie informatiche stavano giocando nel mondo del lavoro. Durante la crisi, ciò che mi procurava maggiore turbamento per non dire vera e propria sofferenza era osservare (insieme ai decessi per decine di migliaia) la perdita dei posti di lavoro e il crollo di varie piccolissime imprese, con l'aggravamento della povertà. Allo stesso momento, però, potevo osservare (e come me tanti) che grazie alle nuove tecnologie una grandissima parte dei lavoratori potevano continuare la loro attività in sicurezza. Grazie a ciò il mondo del lavoro non è crollato. è a questo punto che, scambiando delle idee con amici e colleghi dell'Università Statale di Milano[2], mi è sorta la domanda: forse le tecnologie ICT sono in grado non solo di difendere il lavoro ma anche di crearlo, trasformandosi nella struttura portante del mercato del lavoro di un domani che comincia oggi.

Tale domanda è diventata un'urgenza morale quando ci siamo trovati di fronte all'ennesimo cambio di governo in Italia. Nel suo discorso davanti alle Camere per ottenere la fiducia, Mario Draghi ha elencato una serie di priorità e punti critici fra i quali emergono lavoro e disoccupazione[3]. In questi settori, secondo

---

Florence, 2021.

[2]In particolare nell'ambito del Centro di Ricerca Interdisciplinare sul Diritto delle Amministrazioni Pubbliche (CERIDAP), diretto dalla prof. Diana-Urania Galetta.

[3]*Le comunicazioni del Presidente del Consiglio, Mario Draghi, al Senato della Repubblica sulle dichiarazioni programmatiche del Governo*, Mercoledì, 17 Febbraio 2021, pubblicate integralmente sul sito della Presidenza del Consiglio dei ministri, http://www.governo.it/it/articolo/le-comunicazion

Draghi, l'Italia è in ritardo e le politiche del lavoro devono diventare centrali, con l'assegno di riallocazione da migliorare e i centri per l'impiego da rafforzare: è grazie al programma dell'Unione europea SURE[4] e all'enorme utilizzo della cassa integrazione che durante la fase più critica gli effetti negativi sono stati mitigati[5]. Il giorno dopo l'ottenimento della fiducia del nuovo governo, l'INPS ha presentato un rapporto dell'Osservatorio sul precariato in cui si evidenzia che per l'effetto dell'emergenza Covid nei dodici mesi che vanno dal novembre 2019 al novembre 2020 sono andati persi 664 mila posti di lavoro, ai quali si aggiungono i 2 milioni di nuove assunzioni in meno rispetto all'anno precedente[6], senza contare i disastrosi effetti economici sulle imprese piccolissime e familiari, che hanno accentuato la povertà di ampi strati: tutto questo nonostante il divieto di licenziamento fosse ancora in vigore, mentre il premier Draghi nel suo discorso guardava con preoccupazione al momento in cui il divieto sarebbe venuto meno, fatto che avrebbe aggravato ulteriormente la situazione[7]. Forse in Italia le conseguenze economiche e sociali dell'emergenza sanitaria si sono fatte sentire più che altrove, ma non c'è dubbio che il fenomeno è generalizzato nell'Unione europea, come anche nel resto del mondo. Vale, quindi, la pena di soffermarsi un momento sul contesto strategico sopranazionale[8],

---

i-del-presidente-draghi-al-senato/16225 (in alternativa vedi l'ampia sintesi di Monica Guerzoni sul Corriere della Sera del 18 febbraio 2021)

[4]Support to mitigate Unemployment Risks in an Emergency.

[5]*Le comunicazioni del Presidente del Consiglio, etc., cit.*

[6]*INPS, Osservatorio sul Precariato – Dati sui nuovi rapporti di lavoro, REPORT MENSILE GENNAIO – NOVEMBRE 2020*, Roma, 10 febbraio 2021 (o in alternativa vedi l'articolo di sintesi di Claudia Voltattorni sul Corriere della Sera del 19 febbraio 2021).

[7]*Le comunicazioni del Presidente del Consiglio, etc., cit.*

[8]Vedi a questo proposito *EPRS, Towards a more resilient Europe post-coronavirus. I: An initial mapping of structural risks facing the EU, PE 653.208, July 2021; II: Capabilities and gaps in the EU's capacity to dress structural risks, PE 652.024, October 2020: III: Options to enhance the EU's resilience to structural risks, PE 659.437, January 2021.*

e non limitare lo sguardo all'Italia.

Ovunque, la disoccupazione determinata dalla crisi pandemica ha colpito in maniera drammatica donne e giovani, con rischi strutturali (disoccupazione a lungo termine) per il futuro: come ho già detto il programma europeo (provvisorio) SURE ha cercato di frenare il fenomeno, ma i rischi per il futuro restano alti. è evidente che ciò comporterà l'aumento della povertà e delle diseguaglianze in strati sociali importanti, secondo alcuni col rischio di raggiungere livelli di insostenibilità. Sul piano europeo sono molte le iniziative adottate per far fronte alla situazione, a partire dall'ormai arcinoto strumento EU Next Generation[9] e dalla flessibilità nell'uso di strumenti come lo EU Solidarity Fund[10], entrambi destinati ad evitare la recessione economica e favorire la ripresa della crescita. Sono cioè iniziative che hanno un effetto indiretto sul lavoro e sull'occupazione. Oltre al già menzionato SURE si segnalano inoltre altre iniziative, come Youth Employment Initiative e Youth Employment Support[11], che si prefiggono di intervenire direttamente sul problema. Tutte queste iniziative sono ovviamente pensate per aiutare gli Stati membri, che a loro volta hanno adottato misure nella stessa direzione facendo crescere considerevolmente deficit e debito pubblico: si tratta, credo, di una bomba a effetto ritardato, che provocherà danni quando non si potrà intervenire nella protezione sociale e nella redistribuzione della ricchezza a causa della mancanza di risorse finanziarie. Allo stato attuale delle cose, il dibattito a livello europeo si orienta verso soluzioni resilienti, come per esempio la trasformazione del Fondo Sociale Europeo in un European "employment" and social fund, insieme alla creazione di

---

[9]Vedi le descrizioni dettagliate sul sito della Commissione europea, https://ec.europa.eu/info/strategy/recovery-plan-europe_en

[10]Vedi le descrizioni dettagliate sul sito della Commissione europea, https://ec.europa.eu/regional_policy/en/funding/solidarity-fund/covid-19

[11]Vedi le descrizioni dettagliate sul sito della Commissione europea, rispettivamente: https://ec.europa.eu/social/main.jsp?catId=1176 e https://ec.europa.eu/social/main.jsp?catId=1036

una Pan-European "employment" agency[12]. Infatti, la riallocazione della forza lavoro sarà certamente uno dei pilastri politici del prossimo futuro: sarà una sfida a livello nazionale, ma sarà decisivo il supporto e l'orientamento europeo.

Tuttavia, pur fondamentali per la resilienza, si tratta comunque di misure di sostegno che hanno bisogno di un intervento strutturale: questo è oggi chiaramente individuato negli investimenti per adeguare l'Europa all'era digitale. Analisi approfondite di organismi internazionali[13] hanno già dimostrato come l'avvento delle tecnologie abbia cambiato i processi di produzione e il mondo del lavoro: quello che sta accadendo è che tutti i mestieri e le professioni subiscono la digitalizzazione come elemento essenziale al loro esercizio, con la conseguenza che anche il mercato del lavoro (domanda-offerta) tiene oramai conto di questa necessità. D'altronde, ed è la seconda conseguenza sul mercato del lavoro, i profili specificamente IT diventano essenziali al funzionamento delle imprese e delle amministrazioni pubbliche. Con la crisi pandemica tale fenomeno si è accentuato e sta aggravando l'asimmetria fra i lavoratori, emarginando progressivamente e rapidamente quelli che hanno una preparazione digitale insufficiente. Una (grande?) parte del mondo del lavoro rischia di perdere le opportunità di impiego che la tecnologia crea; alcuni lavoratori stanno addirittura perdendo già ora l'impiego a causa di tale deficit formativo. C'è inoltre un problema capitale: i paesi europei sono ancora largamente dipendenti dalle tecnologie prodotte da altri altrove. Il primo obiettivo è riuscire a creare quella che ormai si chiama "sovranità digitale" euro-

---

[12]Sulla European employment strategy, vedi ampiamente il sito della Commissione europea, https://ec.europa.eu/social/main.jsp?catId=101&l angId=en

[13]Mi riferisco a *ESPAS Report 2019: Global Trends to 2030*, *World Economic Forum 2020: COVID -19 Risks Outlook – A Preliminary Mapping and Its Implications, 2020*, *OECD Employment Outlook 2019: The Future of Work, 2019*, and *Eurofound: Living, working and COVID-19 – First findings – April 2020*.

pea: intelligenza artificiale, quantum computing, infrastrutture per il data cloud, micro-electronics, internet of things, connettività 5G, piattaforme per e-commerce, video-conferencing, social networks[14]. È incredibile quanto ampiamente sia ignorato, oppure (se conosciuto) quanto sia trascurato il fatto che tutti questi strumenti assolutamente necessari all'economia e al lavoro siano tutti in mani extra-europee. Com'è noto, per fronte alla situazione l'Unione europea ha varato progressivamente un'*Agenda digitale europea,* un *Mercato unico digitale* e ultimamente un programma chiamato *Plasmare il futuro digitale dell'Europa*[15]: è questo il quadro in cui bisogna agire, in una sinergia tra livelli nazionali e livello europeo perché la crisi pandemica ha messo in luce l'ampiezza del ritardo degli investimenti nel digitale sia sul piano delle imprese (soprattutto piccole e medie) che delle pubbliche amministrazioni. Nei sette obiettivi strategici del programma del nuovo governo Draghi si ritrova un capitolo dedicato a "innovazione e cablaggio[16]" che apre le porte alla Transizione digitale e al rafforzamento delle infrastrutture: per queste ultime gli interventi sulla banda larga e sul 5G appaiono nel programma di governo come prioritari[17]. Il che è assolutamente pertinente, purché nell'attuazione ci si riferisca chiaramente al contesto strategico europeo (cosa di cui non c'è motivo di dubitare). Ma quello che pare di grande importanza è l'idea che la transizione digitale sarà "trasversale" alle competenze di vari ministeri e sarà il pilastro della riforma della Pubblica amministrazione.

---

[14]L'utilizzo della terminologia inglese si giustifica per entrata ormai nell'uso comune del linguaggio, in alcune lingue anche in maniera ufficializzata.

[15]*Agenda digitale europea,* COM(2010)245 final, Bruxelles, 19.5.2010; *Mercato unico digitale,* COM(2015)192 final, Bruxelles, 6.5.2015; *Plasmare il futuro digitale dell'Europa,* COM(2020)67 final, 19.2.2020.

[16]*Le comunicazioni del Presidente del Consiglio, etc., cit.* (o in alternativa vedi l'ampia sintesi di Marco Galluzzo sul Corriere della Sera del 15 febbraio 2021).

[17]Ibidem.

Anche questo approccio appare pertinente: la speranza è che nella trasversalità dell'azione si ponga al centro di tutto e di tutti l'impatto sul mercato del lavoro che si sta configurando.

Oltre al digitale, vi sono due fattori che arricchiscono le potenzialità individuali sul nuovo mercato del lavoro che sta emergendo con rapidità impressionante: ancora una volta bisogna usare la terminologia inglese che è quella invalsa, lo Upskilling (che possiamo tradurre con "riqualificazione delle proprie competenze") e il Soft Skills (che possiamo tradurre con "capacità e attitudini collaterali"). Nel primo caso, Upskilling, si tratta di una sfida primordiale tanto per i lavoratori quanto per le imprese e le amministrazioni pubbliche. Aggiornare e arricchire le proprie competenze, ma anche sviluppare nuove attitudini al fine di migliorare le performance nel luogo di lavoro (imprese e amministrazioni) e/o essere attrattivi nel mercato del lavoro: evidentemente l'innovazione tecnologica è il fattore di pressione principale in questo senso. Peraltro, dall'inizio della pandemia si è osservato ovunque un fenomeno a prima vista bizzarro ma in realtà comprensibile: il numero di lavoratori che hanno riflettuto seriamente alla possibilità di cambiare lavoro è considerevolmente aumentato. Ebbene, lo Upskilling favorisce la riuscita del cambiamento e riduce i processi di obsolescenza delle competenze. Nel caso del Soft Skills si tratta piuttosto di un rafforzamento delle proprie capacità professionali, ovvero di un sostegno contestuale solido alla propria specializzazione. Oramai nei processi di ricerca e di assunzione del personale i manager responsabili delle risorse umane richiedono prioritariamente le seguenti qualità umane e morali: per le prime, creatività, persuasione, collaborazione, adattabilità e intelligenza emozionale; per le seconde, integrità, responsabilità, simpatia, gestione del tempo, autocontrollo e flessibilità. Per completare il quadro, infine, ci pare occorra inoltre qualcosa che il mondo contemporaneo ha represso in maniera seria a causa dei meccanismi di sopravvivenza che si sono imposti: si tratta della Positività, cioè l'atteggiamento positivo di fronte a situazioni che alimentano la solitudine, l'incertezza e l'angoscia. Dalle cose semplici come contatti virtuali divertenti, adeguamento dei ritmi di lavoro e passeggiate quotidiane, fino ai processi di apprendimento della positività organizzati da imprese e amministrazioni pubbliche. è un atteggiamento da coltivare e curare, che ha una ricaduta immediata sulla resilienza e la capacità di reazione del lavoratore.

A questo punto ci sono abbastanza elementi per concludere le presenti riflessioni. Il governo Draghi è entrato in funzione in un momento di grande trasformazione del mercato del lavoro, caratterizzato dalla determinante influenza delle tecnologie informatiche e da un grado elevato di mobilità. L'emergenza della pandemia, in corso da quasi un anno al momento del giuramento del governo Draghi, si è abbattuta sul mercato del lavoro con distruzione di posti e mancata creazione di nuovi, accentuando allo stesso tempo i menzionati processi in corso (digitale, mobilità). Il fenomeno è però sopranazionale e l'Unione europea sta intervenendo su due piani, far fronte all'emergenza (SURE, Youth Initiative, EU Next Generation etc.) e intervenire sulla base di una strategia: la risposta strategica è chiaramente incentrata sull'investimento nelle tecnologie informatiche. Sono queste ultime infatti che stanno modificando i processi di produzione e l'esercizio di mestieri e professioni, che stanno ridisegnando il mercato del lavoro con l'imposizione della riqualificazione dei lavoratori e la presenza dei profili IT, che stanno creando una forte asimmetria fra i lavoratori e le loro prospettive di impiego. Il discorso del Premier e il programma di governo tengono conto del problema: da un lato annunciano riforme per l'assegno di riallocazione e per i centri per l'impiego, dall'altro menzionano il rafforzamento delle infrastrutture (banda larga, 5G) e la trasversalità della transizione digitale. Il che appare adeguato. La speranza è che tutto questo sia fatto nel contesto strategico europeo e che il mercato del lavoro diventi il perno onnipresente della transizione trasversale.

English Summary

During the Covid emergency, I dealt with the role which technologies, in particular ICTs, are coming to play in today's world, with a particular focus on the functioning of democracy:[1] the functioning of parliamentary and representative institutions in general and likewise citizens' oversight of what was happening were made possible by these technologies. However, the equally important role that information technologies were playing in the world of work did not escape me either. What was disturbing and distressing to me was to observe (along with the tens of thousands of deaths) the loss of jobs and the collapse of a number of very small businesses, dragging people deeper into poverty: at the same time, however, I could see that thanks to the new technologies a very large number of workers could continue to work safely. Thanks to this, the world of work did not collapse.

Everywhere, unemployment caused by the pandemic crisis has dramatically hit women and young people, entailing structural risks (long-term unemployment) for the future: the European SURE programme[2] has tried to curb this, but the risks for the future remain high. Many initiatives have been taken to address the situation, starting with the well-known EU Next Generation instrument[3] and flexibility in the use of instruments such as the EU Solidarity Fund[4], both of which are designed to stave off economic recession and foster the resumption of growth. These are initiatives that have an indirect positive effect on work

---

[1] In particular with the publication G. Vilella, *eDemocracy. Dove ci porta la democrazia digitale*, Pendragon, Bologna, 2020, and G. Vilella, *The European Parliament Administration facing the challenge of eDemocracy*, European Press Academic Publishing, Florence, 2021.

[2] Support to mitigate Unemployment Risks in an Emergency.

[3] https://ec.europa.eu/info/strategy/recovery-plan-europe_en

[4] https://ec.europa.eu/regional_policy/en/funding/solidarity-fund/covid-19

and employment. Other initiatives, such as the Youth Employment Initiative and Youth Employment Support[5], aim to have a direct impact. As things stand, the debate at European level is tending towards resilient solutions, such as the transformation of the European Social Fund into a European *employment* and social fund, together with the creation of a Pan-European *employment* agency.[6]

However, while fundamental for resilience, these are support measures which need further structural intervention: the latter is now clearly identified in investments to adapt Europe to the digital era. In-depth analyses by international bodies[7] have already shown how the advent of technologies has changed production processes and the world of work: what is happening is that all trades and professions are being digitised with digitisation being an essential part of how they are practised, with the result that the labour market (supply and demand) is now also taking this need into account. Moreover, and this is the second consequence for the labour market, IT-specific profiles are becoming essential for the functioning of businesses and public administrations. With the pandemic crisis, this need has become more pronounced whilst at the same time exacerbating the asymmetry between workers by progressively and rapidly marginalising those with insufficient digital training. Part of the world of work risks losing the employment opportunities that technology creates, while some workers are already losing their jobs because of this training deficit. There is also a major problem: European countries are still largely dependent on technologies produced by

---

[5]https://ec.europa.eu/social/main.jsp?catId=1176 and https://ec.europa.eu/social/main.jsp?catId=1036

[6]https://ec.europa.eu/social/main.jsp?catId=101&langId=en

[7]I refer to *ESPAS Report 2019: Global Trends to 2030, World Economic Forum 2020: COVID -19 Risks Outlook – A Preliminary Mapping and Its Implications, 2020, OECD Employment Outlook 2019: The Future of Work, 2019,* and *Eurofound: Living, working and COVID-19 – First findings – April 2020.*

others elsewhere. The first goal is to create what is now called European "digital sovereignty": artificial intelligence, quantum computing, data cloud infrastructure, micro-electronics, internet of things, 5G connectivity, e-commerce platforms, videoconferencing, social networks. It is unbelievable how largely ignored, or (if known) how neglected it is that all these tools which are absolutely necessary for the economy and work are all in non-European hands. As we know, in response to this situation, the European Union has progressively launched a *Digital Agenda for Europe*, a *Digital Single Market* and, most recently, a programme called *Shaping Europe's Digital Future*:[8] this is the framework within which we need to act, with a synergy between national and European levels, because the pandemic crisis has brought to light the extent to which investment in digital technology is lagging behind both in businesses (especially small and medium-sized undertakings) and in public administrations.

There are also two factors that enrich individual potential in the new labour market which is emerging with impressive speed: Upskilling and Soft Skills. In the first case, Upskilling, it is an essential challenge for workers as much as for businesses and public administrations. Updating and enriching one's skills, but also developing new aptitudes in order to improve performance in the workplace (businesses and administrations) and/or to be attractive in the labour market: technological innovation is clearly the main factor pressing in this direction. Moreover, since the beginning of the pandemic, a phenomenon has been observed everywhere which is at first sight strange but in reality understandable: the number of workers who have given serious thought to the possibility of changing jobs has increased considerably. Well, Upskilling promotes successful change and reduces the process of skills obsolescence. In the case of Soft Skills, it is more a question of strengthening one's professional skills or of providing solid

---

[8] COM(2010)245 final, Brussels, 19.5.2010; COM(2015)192 final, Brussels, 6.5.2015; COM(2020)67 final, 19.2.2020, respectively.

contextual support for one's specialisation. Nowadays, in the processes of recruitment and hiring, human resource managers require the following human and moral qualities as a priority: the former are creativity, persuasion, collaboration, adaptability and emotional intelligence; the latter, integrity, responsibility, sympathy, time management, self-control and flexibility. Finally, to complete the picture, it seems to me that something is needed that the contemporary world has seriously repressed on account of the survival mechanisms which have been required: positivity, that is, a positive attitude in the face of situations which make for loneliness, uncertainty and anxiety: this is an attitude to be cultivated and nurtured, which has an immediate impact on the worker's resilience and ability to react.

To conclude, therefore, the European Union is acting on two levels: tackling the emergency (SURE, Youth Initiative, EU Next Generation, etc.) and launching a strategy focused on investment in information technologies. It is these technologies which are changing production processes and the practice of trades and professions, reshaping the labour market by necessitating retraining for workers and the presence of IT profiles and creating a strong asymmetry between workers and their employment prospects.

Chapter 4

Second half of the ninth legislature: challenges and potential opportunities for the European Union

Rivista Interdisciplinare sul Diritto delle Amministrazioni Pubbliche

Fascicolo 3/2021

Luglio – Settembre

Abstract (Italian): *Quando l'Unione Europea tornerà dopo la pausa estiva (la rentrée), nel settembre 2021, inizierà la seconda metà della nona legislatura e la seconda metà del mandato della Commissione europea presieduta da Ursula von der Leyen: le sfide sono enormi, i progetti in corso sono numerosi e complessi e tutte le istituzioni europee sono chiamate a far fronte a una situazione certo delicata ma ricca di stimoli e potenzialità. Innanzitutto, la Conferenza sul futuro dell'Europa deve essere portata a termine con successo: qui è in gioco non solo la credibilità dell'Unione, ma anche la sua capacità di tenere saldamente il timone nei prossimi anni. Allo stesso tempo, ma sempre strettamente legata alla Conferenza, c'è la questione della difesa dei valori fondanti dell'Unione, in particolare lo stato di diritto e la non discriminazione, che sono oggetto di controversie con alcuni Stati. C'è poi la necessità di far partire l'operazione Next Generation EU – una delle più importanti iniziative politiche ed economiche della storia del continente – e, con essa, far uscire l'Europa dalla crisi pandemica, che coinvolge diverse questioni oltre a quella, evidente, della salute. I prossimi anni saranno decisivi anche per valutare la validità e la solidità dell'accordo sulla Brexit, delicato come le tensioni sulla libera circolazione determinate dall'emergenze. Infine, c'è l'immenso cantiere della digitalizzazione con i suoi vari temi (intelligenza artificiale, servizi digitali, telelavoro, cyber sicurezza). Vale quindi la pena di fare rapidamente il punto della situazione in corso.*

When the European Union will come back after the summer break (la rentrée) in September 2021, the second half of the ninth legislature will begin, along with the second half of the term of office of the European Commission presided over by Ursula von der Leyen: the challenges are huge and the projects and unfinished business under way are numerous and complex and all the European institutions are being called upon to cope with a situation which is admittedly delicate yet full of stimuli and potential. First of all, the Conference on the Future of Europe must be brought to a successful conclusion: here not only is the Union's credibility at stake but also the question of its ability to keep a steady hand on the tiller in the years ahead. At the same time, but still closely linked to the Conference, there is the question of defending the founding values of the Union, in particular the rule of law and non-discrimination, which are the subject of disputes with some States. Then there is the need to get the Next Generation EU operation – one of the most important political and economic initiatives in the continent's history – off on the right track and, with it, get Europe out of the pandemic crisis, which has a variety of aspects in addition to the obvious one of health. The next few years will also be decisive for assessing the validity and solidity of the agreement on Brexit, which is as sensitive as the pressures on free movement brought about by emergencies. Lastly, there is the immense construction site of digitalisation with its various themes (artificial intelligence, Digital Service, teleworking, cybersecurity). It is therefore worth quickly taking stock of where we stand.

4.1 The Conference on the Future of Europe

The Conference on the Future of Europe was officially launched in Strasbourg on 9 May 2021, Europe Day, much later than originally planned on account not only of the pandemic but also of the gruelling negotiations. The French President, Emmanuel Macron, opened the proceedings with a highly significant speech. He stressed the Union's chief weakness of lacking the capacity to decide quickly and resolutely, while pointing to the defeatism, lassitude and careless impatience to which Covid-19 had given rise. He went on to recall the need for determination to defend the sovereignty of the European space: something that is achieved by the existence of creators and producers in Europe. On the other hand, he recalled that Europe is a model in various regions of the world on account of its solidarity. Macron drew attention to the fact that, during the pandemic, Europe, more than in any other region of the world, had prioritised life and guaranteed the functioning of democracy in the face of all the sirens of authoritarianism.

At this point, it is worth giving a very brief account of how the "formal" debate unfolded over time: after the idea had been launched by President Macron,[1] Ursula von der Leyen took up the proposal in her speech on the guidelines for the European Commission made to the European Parliament on 16 July 2019 before her election as President.[2] Subsequently, the European Parliament adopted a first resolution on the topic on 15 January 2020,[3] which was followed by the Commission's Communication of 22 January 2020.[4] Parliament returned to the subject with a resolution on 18 June 2020[5] and finally the Council adopted a common position on 24 June 2020.[6] On

---

[1]Immediately after his election, on several occasions and most notably during a keynote speech in Berlin.

[2]Opening Statement in the European Parliament Plenary Session by Ursula von der Leyen, Candidate for President of the European Commission (europa.eu)

[3]European Parliament resolution of 15 January 2020 on the position of the European Parliament on the Conference on the Future of Europe, P9_TA(2020)0010, https://www.europarl.europa.eu/doceo/document/TA-9-2020-0010_EN.html

[4]Communication from the Commission to the European Parliament and the Council shaping the Conference on the Future of Europe, 22.1.2020, COM(2020) 27 final, https://eur-lex.europa.eu/legal-content/EN/TXT/?uri=CELEX%3A52020DC0027.

[5]European Parliament resolution of 18 June 2020 on the European Parliament's position on the Conference on the Future of Europe, P9 TA(2020)0153, https://www.europarl.europa.eu/doceo/document/TA-9-2020-0153_EN.html

[6]Presidency of the Council of the European Union, Conference on the Future of Europe, AG32 INST120, Brussels, 24 June 2020, setting out in

this basis, the practicalities could be negotiated and the conference launched.

The Conference Plenary (433 members) is scheduled to work for a year with a mandate to take into account the contributions of the citizens, who are to be consulted on a large scale, and then hand over the results to Macron himself, who was the first promoter of the initiative, in March 2022 during the French Presidency of the Council. The official presidency of the conference is made up of the presidents of the three institutions, but there is an *Executive Board* chaired by representatives of the three institutions which is take care of the practical management of the whole machine on a permanent footing. The first meeting of the Conference Plenary took place on 19 June 2021, and thereafter the programme envisages at least one meeting per month. The Plenary also divided up the work by forming 9 working groups.

A digital platform had already been opened on 19 April, receiving a large number of contributions from the outset: the declared aim was to prevent the discussion from being taken over by "the usual suspects" repeating their already familiar positions. According to the first internal "activity report" of the Conference, prepared and circulated in July 2021,[7] the citizen participation aspect, the supreme objective of the Conference, got off to a good start with 19,000 participants registered on the platform, 5,000 ideas, over 10,000 comments and more than 29,000 "endorsements of ideas", with almost 1 million people having visited the platform. This was considered a good start, but it was clear that more citizens should be reached. In terms of the content of the first online debates, the words most closely associated with today's Union were *solidarity, unity and cooperation*, while the words associated with tomorrow's Union were *hope and challenges*.

---

detail the Council position as agreed at the Permanent Representative Committee, https://www.consilium.europa.eu/media/44679/st09102-en20.pdf

[7]POLITICO Brussels Playbook, 30 July 2021, https://www.politico.eu/newsletter/brussels-playbook/politico-brussels-playbook-time-to-say-goodbye-no-eulogies-though-over-and-out/

4.2   Rule of law

The Commission's first Report on the Rule of Law in the European Union was presented in September 2020,[8] focusing on the processes of democratic backsliding, together with the concept of the European "way of life": rule of law, democracy, and fundamental rights. The report addresses four areas that are examined for each EU member country: the justice system, the anti-corruption framework, media pluralism, and institutional issues related to checks and balances. On top of this, the emergency measures adopted for the pandemic are considered.

The Commission has adopted a participatory and consultative method: discussion with the Member States (network of national contact points) and written contributions from stakeholders and civil society. The evaluations are made on the basis of a consistent and comparable approach for all States: in addition to the general communication, specific reports are presented for each State.

A major dispute has long been going on between the Commission, on the one hand, and Hungary and Poland, on the other.[9] After a hearing in December 2018 on the situation in Poland and a hearing in December 2019 on the situation in Hungary, the Council of Ministers did not return to the subject until much later in June 2021: the Commission considered it absolutely necessary to continue with the Article 7 procedure because (Commissioner Jourová argued) the things that had happened in the meantime had only increased concerns. In addition, there was concern about the governments' wait-and-see attitude.

---

[8]2020 Rule of law report – Communication and country chapters, https://ec.europa.eu/info/publications/2020-rule-law-report-communication-and-country-chapters_en. However, it is important to remind that the process for the application of art. 7 to Hungary has been opened by the European Parliament.

[9]Even for Romania, at one point, the issue of legislative interventions not respecting the rule of law had been raised with regard to projects to reform the judiciary and the Criminal Code, including the downsizing of the Anti-Corruption Agency: see *Le Soir*, 14-15 August 2018. But after protests in the country and remonstrances by Commissioner Jourová, no more came of the matter.

After an intense debate on these issues; the Commission proposed introducing the principle that access to EU funds should be conditional on respect for the rule of law. In November 2020, Hungary and Poland vetoed making access to resources for economic growth (Next Generation EU) conditional on respect for the principle of the rule of law: the veto opposed the budget, as it could not be used against the specific legislative act.[10] The European Parliament voted for conditionality in December 2020, accepting what has been called the "Merkel compromise", the German presidency's mediation proposal: the Commission must first find that the principles of the rule of law have been violated and then propose cutting or freezing EU funds. After that, however, it is the Council that votes by a qualified majority on the proposals made by the Commission. Although some have referred to this as giving in, in truth this provision is a major revolution in the history of the EU. As expected (it was part of the compromise), Poland and Hungary raised the question of the legitimacy of the principle of conditionality before the Court of Justice,[11] with not only the result that the implementation of the regulation was blocked[12], but also the risk identified by many that the Court's judicial activity would be "politicised".

As a matter of fact, this risk is actually already present in the pending proceedings on the application of the Article 7 procedure and other aspects concerning mainly Poland: this country is accused in various quarters of turning its democratic system into an authoritarian "democracy" because of interventions with respect to the Constitutional Court, the independence of the judicial system, public companies and media, and private media. The CJEU rejected Poland's new rules on Supreme Court judges in July 2021 and ordered changes to their provisions, but the Polish Constitutional Court questioned

---

[10]Regulation (EU, Euratom) 2020/2092 of the European Parliament and of the Council of 16 December 2020 on a general regime of conditionality for the protection of the Union budget, OJ L 433I, 22.12.2020, p. 1.

[11]Case C-156/21 *Hungary v. European Parliament and Council*, OJ C 138, 19.4.2021, p. 24; Case C-157/21 *Poland v. European Parliament and Council*, OJ 138, 19.4.2021, p. 26.

[12]Indeed; in this way the EC cannot adopt the "guidelines" until the end of the judicial process.

the primacy of EU law, arguing that the CJEU had no competence in the matter. For its part, the Commission formally called on Poland to comply with the CJEU's ruling: otherwise, infringement proceedings would once again be initiated. It should not be forgotten that in June 2021 the Commission had brought infringement proceedings against Germany on account of the well-known ruling of the German Constitutional Court which called in question the CJEU's ruling on the powers of the European Central Bank.[13] The Commission challenged the failure to respect the principle of the primacy of Union law and asked Germany to find a solution. In addition to posing legal problems, the ruling of the Court in Karlsruhe has set a catastrophic precedent in the context of the ongoing proceedings against Poland and Hungary.

A very relevant incident took place in June 2021 on the occasion of the adoption of a proposal for a law in Hungary for the protection of children, explicitly designed to curtail or eliminate the rights of homosexuals and other sexual orientations: in a widely circulated official statement,[14] the President of the Commission called the Hungarian bill "a shame" on the ground that it was contrary to the fundamental rights enshrined in the European Charter and the Treaties, and announced that the Commission had sent a formal letter warning of legal proceedings should the bill be enacted. The Hungarian government officially responded[15] by saying that it was President Van der

---

[13]For an in-depth analysis, see Diana-Urania Galetta, *Karlsruhe über alles? The reasoning on the principle of proportionality in the judgment of 5 May 2020 of the German BVerfG and its consequences*, and Jacques Ziller, *The unbearable heaviness of the German constitutional judge. On the judgment of the Second Chamber of the German Federal Constitutional Court of 5 May 2020 concerning the European Central Bank's PSPP programme*, both in CERIDAP 2/2020, at https://ceridap.eu/.

[14]European Commission, Statement by European Commission President on the new Hungarian bill that discriminates against people based on their sexual orientation, Brussels, 23 June 2021, https://ec.europa.eu/commission/presscorner/detail/en/STATEMENT_21_3164.

[15]See *Hungary's anti-LGBT law is a "shame" says Ursula von der Leyen*, Euronews, 23 June 2021, https://www.euronews.com/2021/06/23/hungary-s-anti-lgbt-law-is-a-shame-says-ursula-von-der-leyen.

Leyen's statement that was a shame because it was based on false allegations and by claiming that the law was inspired by the Charter of Fundamental Rights and that von der Leyen's remarks constituted a political opinion without a previously conducted, impartial inquiry. This incident between the Commission and Hungary led to a serious debate among Member States. The vast majority of the members of the European Council openly criticised the proposed Hungarian legislation as contrary to Community values, some even went so far as to say that Hungary was now outside the Union: however, it must be noted that support for this view was not unanimous and margins of uncertainty remained.

The Vice-President of the Commission responsible for "promoting our European way of life", Margaritis Schinas saw fit to intervene in an important interview[16] to underline the relevance of the "open and clear" debate that had taken place at the European Council: it was, according to Schinas, the first time that these issues had been addressed at the highest level in such a direct way and therefore that the problem had been laid on the table. For Schinas, there is a *corpus europeum* which is the soul of European values and the foundation for our way of life. The President of the European Parliament, David Maria Sassoli, also reacted by sending a long and detailed letter to the President of the Commission, which was made public.[17] Although this letter does not actually refer to the new Hungarian legislation, it does stress the fact that respect for the rule of law has deteriorated in some European countries. The objective of the letter was to urge the Commission, in relatively strong terms, to act for the immediate application of the regulation on the conditionality of financial flows on respect for the principles of the rule of law. Recalling the official positions of the European Parliament,[18] the letter denounces

---

[16] *Notre mode de vie est le meilleur bouclier contre les dérives*, *Le Soir*, 30 June 2021.

[17] The letter can be accessed here: https://cdn.g4media.ro/wp-content/uploads/2021/06/Sassoli-Letter-EC-230621.pdf

[18] Resolution of 17 December 2020, P9_TA(2020)0360; Resolution of 25 March 2021, P9_TA(2021)0103; and Resolution of 10 June 2021, P9_TA(2021)0287.

the fact that no action has been taken several months after the regulation's entry into force notwithstanding the obvious problems of non-compliance with European principles. Lastly, in July 2021, the Commission initiated infringement proceedings against Poland and Hungary[19] for their anti-LGBTIQ measures because, the Commission claims, they discriminate against citizens on the basis of their sexual orientation. At the end of July, the Hungarian Prime Minister Viktor Orbán announced a series of referendums on the contested provisions and announced that he would renounce Recovery Plan funds (€7.2 billion) if they were conditional on the abolition of the controversial LGBTIQ law.

In short, the conflict on the importance and the conception of the founding values of the EU and liberal democracy, both of which are opposed by Hungary and Poland, and likewise Slovenia (which took over the Council Presidency in July 2021), is becoming very serious: I do not believe that this issue can be sidestepped during the Conference on the Future of Europe.

4.3   Recovery (Next Generation EU)

The emergence of Covid-19 affected the activity of the EU as a whole, since everything is interconnected: when it was realised that, because of the measures being taken (including the lockdown), the problem was no longer only one of health, but was becoming a colossal economic problem, the Member States showed that they could not agree, or in any event had no method for reaching agreement quickly, whilst, in contrast, the supranational institutions exhibited a great capacity to react and decide[20]. The President of the Commission, Ursula von der Leyen, presented her proposals to the Plenary of the European

---

[19]The Commission also brought proceedings against Hungary in the CJEU for unlawfully restricting access to the asylum procedure. https://ec.europa.eu/commission/presscorner/detail/en/ip_21_3424

[20]Many are the concrete and urgent measures adopted at the EU level, but the most emblematic (a real victory) is the Green Pass harmonised for all the Member States.

Parliament on 27 May 2020, after the European Council meeting by videoconference on 23 April 2020 had instructed her to prepare a plan "also using innovative instruments". The Commission's plan had various aspects,[21] the central one being the creation of a fund to boost the economy called "Next Generation EU": this is a €750 billion fund financed by recourse to the financial markets, to be repaid over 30 years through the Community budget, which is to be reinforced. It is important to stress that this measure more than "innovative" is really revolutionary in the EU approach, because it reverse and cancel the fundamental principle of no-debt is accepted in the EU finances. Other parallel actions, such as a new European health programme, will accompany the "Next Generation EU" fund. Obviously, the adoption of the MFF (Multiannual Financial Framework) for the period 2021-27,[22] with a ceiling of €1074.3 billion, was decisive in order to be able to add the €750 billion of the recovery plan. The ratification process by all EU Member States was completed at the end of May 2021 (by which time 19 national recovery plans had already been delivered, including the Italian[23]). The national plans are obviously an essential prerequisite for the activation of the funds (which in 2021 became €807 billion after adjustment for inflation). In the second half of June, the Commission had already approved a large proportion of the plans and, in order to underline the historical importance of the event, President von der Leyen went in person to the capitals of the countries concerned to present the approved plan together with the (analytical) point of view of the Commission. In the meantime, on 15 June 2021, the Commission had issued its first bonds on the market,

---

[21]See *European Recovery Plan*, https://ec.europa.eu/info/live-work-trav el-eu/health/coronavirus-response/recovery-plan-europe_it

[22]The interinstitutional agreement (EP, Council, EC) was reached in November 2020 after long and arduous negotiations. The first budget of the new MFF, for 2021, amounts to just over €166 billion, or 1.19% of EU GDP.

[23]The references to Italy are not made because of the author's nationality, but in consideration of the fact that Italy is defined as the essential fulcrum and supporting pillar of the whole operation of relaunching the European economy: this statement has been repeated several times by the President of the Commission.

for a total of €20 billion, in a fully successful operation: it was the first time in the history of the EU.

The Commission will launch its bonds on the markets to finance the recovery plans and repay the loan by 2050 from the European budget, which should either be reinforced by the Member States or be given the benefit of new own taxes on the environment, financial transactions or web enterprises. The funds are to be disbursed in the form of either loans or grants, but according to the guidelines must do no harm to the environment, but rather invest in climate protection, and invest in digitalisation. In any case, what is involved must be predominantly investment and not current expenditure. In addition, the Commission requires some structural reforms relating to the situation of individual countries: for example, Italy is required to do the following: complete the reform of its public administration; strengthen the "spending review"; reform its justice system; adjust mechanisms for managing insolvencies; reform public procurement; undertake digital training and interventions on the labour market, including support for the employment of young people and women; make interventions in the energy and tourism sectors; combat corruption and tax evasion. The Italian plan was also approved by the Commission in June 2021, with a very positive assessment, apart from the cost analysis (an observation which applies to almost all the national plans approved). What must be clear is that the funding responds to a strategic plan of the Union designed to change the European economy and society to make them more efficient, fairer and more sustainable.

At this point, however, a new chapter opens up, or rather calls to be opened! The many measures taken at European level include the suspension of the Stability Pact on budgetary equilibrium decided autonomously by the European Commission, together with the greater flexibility granted, again by the Commission, to state aid policy. And to think that in February 2020, just before the outbreak of the pandemic, the Commission had launched a debate on the rules of financial rigour in state budgets.[24] The debate is now in the freezer:

---

[24]According to the Commission, the Stability Pact could be assessed as generally positive at that time, as there had been a substantial improvement in the financial situation of the member countries.

the suspension of strict budgetary rules for the Member States owing to the pandemic was probably the decision that prevented the collapse of the European economies;[25] however, this opened the way to a huge problem for the near future, namely public debt of enormous proportions which will have to be dealt with in order not to have a dramatic downside: obviously the situations will not be the same, but in some countries they will be really difficult. If we take Italy once again, its public debt as a percentage of GDP has progressed as follows: 2017, 134.1%; 2018, 134.4; 2019, 134.6; 2020: 155.8! These figures are not simply worrying, looking forward, they are frightening: just think that, Italy's public debt reached a new record of 2.7 trillion euros in June 2021and was about to exceed the threshold of 160% of GDP by the end of the year.

4.4 Brexit

Then there is Brexit. The negotiations were pursued in a very negative climate, with great difficulties and times which seemed to constitute a breaking point: I believe that it was the goodwill of the EU and its negotiator, Michel Barnier, which saved the situation, even if at a certain point the Commission was obliged to bring proceedings against the United Kingdom for "breach" of the withdrawal agreement, accusing it of bad faith in October 2020[26]. An insightful observation

---

[25]It is true that the average recession recorded in 2020 for the European Union was -6.1% with peaks for countries such as Spain (-10.8), Italy (-8.9) and France (-8.7), but already in 2021 growth should be considerable.

[26]The criticism of the UK's handling of Brexit has not only come from the European Commission or other EU institutions, but also from many observers; who have focused on the domestic factors which culminated in the fall of Prime Minister Theresa May, ousted by her own party. But from our point of view it is important to recall the story of the "advice" given by the new Prime Minister Johnson to the Queen that led to the prorogation of the British Parliament for a few weeks: an abnormal measure (!) which was declared to be null and void by the Supreme Court, which held the "advice" to be unlawful because it contained no reasonable justification, and invited Parliament to resume its activities: *R (on the application of*

was made by J. Ziller,[27] who, after making a thorough appraisal of the text of the agreement, found that there is a clear lack of trust between the two parties, while on the part of the UK there is "a dramatic obsession with the European Court of Justice": in this context, Ziller finds, both sides are losers with the main losers being the citizens. The UK has insisted on totally withdrawing from any kind of cooperation in foreign, defence and development policy, and has also emblematically withdrawn from the Erasmus programme. The EU, on the other hand, sought to guarantee maintenance of the principle of non-regression on social issues and the principle of fair competition in trade relations, without social or fiscal dumping: for the EU these are inalienable principles which could trigger withdrawal from the agreement.

The European Parliament took more time before giving the green light to the agreement and the period of provisional application was (unusually) extended: but then ratification arrived, with 660 votes in favour, 5 against and 32 abstentions. Yet the start of the new agreements was not the most peaceful, especially with regard to the movement of persons, residents' rights and fishing, not to mention Northern Ireland. As for the reactions of economic actors, in particular those in the City, at the time of ratification in April 2021, 440 financial institutions were to be transferred (in whole or in part) to European financial centres (Dublin, Paris, Frankfurt, Luxembourg) for a total of £1 trillion and 7,400 jobs: but the figures were incomplete and the game is still on.

4.5   Pressures on freedom of movement

The pandemic, illegal immigration and terrorism (including "homegrown" terrorism by individuals) are constantly bringing pressure to

---

Miller) v. Prime Minister [2019] UKSC 41.

[27]Jacques Ziller, *Brexit: to have or not to have a deal? (first episode) – The New Brexit Deal: Predictable Outcome of a Lose-Lose Negotiation. A First Glance Assessment of the EU-UK Trade Agreement 24.12.2020 (second episode)* CERIDAP, 4/2020.

bear on the regime of free movement at the internal borders: there have been repeated incidents of border closures or threats of closures. Cooperation between Member States in controlling internal borders is considered to fall far short of needs and plans and is proceeding too slowly.

As far as the pandemic is concerned, Covid-19 caused real "shocks" to the EU, because once again the Member States went it alone in combating an epidemic that later became a pandemic, only to discover that there was a real need for at least EU coordination, which was initially left aside. The EU has no powers of its own in the field of health, but may play a very important coordinating and harmonising role, provided that there is cooperation and consensus on the part of the Member States. The fact is, however, that the Member States initially took measures that should not have been unilateral, such as closing borders or bans on the export of medical equipment: these are areas where the Union has strong powers.

With regard to immigration, according to the Commissioner responsible, Ylva Johansson, 3 million legal immigrants and only 140,000 illegal immigrants arrive in Europe every year, whilst 1.5 million leave Europe every year: basically, this would be a fairly balanced situation,[28] even if the public perception is totally different.[29] However, it is clear that the need to focus on illegal immigrants and, more generally, on knowing who is entering European territory remains fundamental: the real issue on the table today is how to improve cooperation between Member States[30] and, even better, which principles should underpin immigration policy, in particular whether we should move beyond the principle of the responsibility of the State of arrival in favour of the concept of asylum seekers or immigration to

---

[28] According to the UNHCR, the years of real crisis were 2015 and 2016, already in 2017 arrivals of migrants in Europe decreased five-fold, and further substantial declines were recorded in the following years.

[29] The case of Italy is very emblematic: the book Istituto Cattaneo, *Immigrazione in Italia: tra realtà e percezione*, Bologna, 2019, shows that 70% of Italians believe that immigrants in Italy account for 25% of the population whilst the true figure is 7%.

[30] The urgence of this aspect emerged once again with the dramatic events of Afghanistan, in august 2021.

Europe (which would revolutionise organisation and procedures).[31]

Lastly, terrorism,[32] despite the fact that it has slowed down, has continued to strike with dramatic and worrying episodes, also in the form of "home-grown" terrorism.[33] This has pushed the problem much further and has meant that freedoms and fundamental rights are now largely sacrificed. The alarm raised by various actors is very high and people are beginning to wonder whether the restrictive measures adopted from time to time should not be called in question: increasingly, recourse is being made to the courts to try to suppress these measures. Some argue that it is also the fault of parliaments which do not adequately scrutinise the rules that are then adopted: the threefold criterion related to the proportionality assessment (suitability, necessity and proportionality in the strict sense) is not paid due attention. Among the many restrictions, there is also the restriction on moving freely within Europe.

The Schengen System[34] is the predestined victim of this: that is why in June 2021 the Commission relaunched a process of reform, while announcing the guiding principles underlying its proposal. These are essentially the strengthening of external borders and police cooperation with exchanges of information, with a view to eliminat-

---

[31] The former president of the Italian Constitutional Court, Valerio Onida, came out strongly in favour of this change of approach in *Corriere della Sera* of 29 August 2019.

[32] Again, there is a problem of cooperation between Member States: for example, an infringement procedure has been initiated by the Commission against Italy for deficiencies in information sharing to combat terrorism and crime.

[33] I would mention here, albeit in passing, two interventions that have touched my sensibilities in this regard: one is by Sabino Cassese, in *Corriere della Sera* of 22 August 2017, who points out that a decisive reaction on the part of the Islamic communities to defeat of this terrorism is still lacking; the other is by the French philosopher Elisabeth Badinter, in *Corriere della Sera* of 4 January 2018, who finds that politicians, because of their anxiety about attracting trouble and their fear of violence, are abandoning our essential principles of the fight against terrorism.

[34] It is redundant but eventually useful to remind that at the beginning it was the Schengen Treaty, which has been integrated in the EU legal system later.

ing all the internal border controls that have multiplied since 2015 and remain substantial in some States. The situation, however, was complicated by the fact that Frontex (the European border control agency) was at that time under pressing criticism even for "violating the fundamental rights" of migrants, not to mention, of course, the divergent positions of the Member States, which prevent compromise and solidarity.

4.6 Digitalisation (and democracy)

This brings me to the chapter on digitalisation, which is very broad and multidimensional. Already in her inaugural speech to the European Parliament, President von der Leyen had stressed that the Union is proud of its values and the rule of law, which are the basis for all action, and that the new Commission intended to relaunch and strengthen European democracy also through the use of all the tools made available by digital democracy: the Commission considers digital democracy to be an essential part of the strengthening of democracy *tout court*. But digitisation is also regarded as a pillar for relaunching the economy and as a sensitive area in the matter of the protection of rights. The new Commission has translated all these aspects into a communication, "Shaping Europe's Digital Future", in which we find the strategy that the Commission intends to follow in the process of the digitisation of Europe, a strategy that develops along three major axes: a technology that works for people; a fair and competitive economy; an open, democratic and sustainable society. The Communication thus offers the strategic framework for complex action which is already under way with the Digital Agenda for Europe, the Digital Internal Market, data protection, copyright protection, taxation of big tech, participatory platforms and electronic money. These are all issues which I have already addressed in depth[35] and will be central to the European Union's action in the

---

[35]Allow me to refer to G. Vilella, *E-Democracy. Dove ci porta la democrazia digitale*, Pendragon, Bologna, 2020, *passim*, so as not to go back over things already said. For the Commission's "digital philosophy",

years to come. Here, however, I want to highlight only the most recent new aspects that have emerged in a consistent manner, including (but not only) as a result of the pandemic emergency. These are the issues that the European Union has launched in recent times.

The first, which is certainly related to the Covid-19 emergency, is cybersecurity. 2020 saw a boom in cybercrimes in the form of ransomware. In August 2021 in Italy, the case of the hacker attack on the Lazio Region with the blocking of data and a demand for ransom (ransomware) broke out: the event gave rise to much emotion everywhere in Europe, but it has been an obvious risk for a long time for the entire Italian administration and beyond. There was talk of terrorism or foreign incursions. The attack is said to have originated from the PC of a smart working employee, which drew attention to the fact that at least one in six hacker attacks originates from remote PCs, shedding light on the fragility of smart working in its current state. Dramatic figures emerged of the ongoing phenomenon, also in private households: in total, there was a 40% increase in 2020 compared with the previous year, but already in the first half of 2021 the increase was 400% when it comes to national IT systems. All this has accelerated the establishment of a Cyber Security Agency in Italy, but it remains clear that the only effective way forward is action at EU level, even if the EU is still struggling compared with China and the US. But the phenomenon has a much larger scope: during the first summit between US President Biden and Russian President Putin (June 2021), the topic of cybersecurity was one of the two main discussion points. Or rather, to be precise, the theme was the cyber-war that is now being fought silently with economic, political and strategic consequences: Russia seems to have developed more ad-

---

see the recent study, *Exploring Digital Government Transformation in the EU – Understanding public sector innovation in a data-driven society*, Misuraca, G., Barcevičius, E. and Codagnone, C. editor(s), EUR 30333 EN, Publications Office of the European Union, Luxembourg, 2020, the final recommendations of which include the need: to build human capacity to ensure a successful Digital Government Transformation, to take advantage of predictive analytics in order to improve policy making and service delivery, and to create a culture of digital transformation within the public sector.

vanced techniques than the US, probably through the use of pirates and privateers, which constitute a barrier to going straight to the institutional level. Propaganda interference, "classical" espionage by computer, ransom demands in various sectors with enormous damage are attributable, according to experts, directly or indirectly to Russia. It is no longer a question of cybercrime, but of national security problems, with operations being handled by large professional criminal organisations, based not only in Russia, but also in African countries or EU Member States.

The second aspect is also linked to the pandemic emergency because it concerns the structural transformations resulting from teleworking to which resort was made in order not to be paralysed by the pandemic. On the basis of the experience gained during the Covid-19 emergency, the Commission has launched a plan to reduce its office buildings by 50% in ten years (by 2030) by reorganising work through teleworking. This will also reduce the institution's carbon footprint. Belgium, like the Commission, has also launched a plan make a drastic reduction in office space for civil servants: the federal level has envisaged the possibility of working two days a week in teleworking and creating coworking spaces for civil servants in order to reduce office space by 200,000 square metres by 2030. The European Parliament has also adopted a system of teleworking, that is very well ruling structured and organised: it foresees three modes of teleworking: standard (one day per week on an average monthly basis), moderate (two days) and maxi (three days). Data protection, health and safety at work outside the Parliament's premises are also taken into account in the decision setting up the teleworking in the EP[36].

Reorganisation of space and reorganisation of the way we work clearly go hand in hand: the issue has been on the table for years, ever since the launch of the so-called NWOW (new way of working), which slowly progressed up to the point of when pandemic broke out. Today we speak of a new normal, which completely changes the old, to which no return can be made. One of the most important consequences is that we have to rethink personnel management, a decisive aspect which adds to the ruling spatial and temporal flexibility: staff

---

[36] 2021.07.16 – SG Decision – New teleworking rules 01.09.2021

can no longer be regarded simply as a resource or human capital, they will need more attention in the new context. It will be necessary to guarantee individual satisfaction, to guarantee empathy in the organisation and to guarantee an appropriate lifestyle: hence, it is the role of the manager which will have to be revisited. But there are also other essential aspects, such as ergonomics, for which new rules on compensation for workers will have to be secured, as is already the case in some countries such as Belgium.

The third aspect I want to mention is not directly related to the pandemic, but has been largely influenced by the growing importance of large IT companies in the pandemic emergency. It was in December 2020 that the Commission, after an extensive consultation process with national, regional and local levels, presented its draft Digital Service Act, by which it aims to regulate the obligations of IT services (GAFAM, above all, and others) that play an intermediary role between the provision of goods or services or content and consumers. The Commission wants to indicate how interested parties can identify and report illegal content, on the one hand, and how companies can take compulsory action to suppress it, on the other. However, this is to only about the obvious incitements to hatred, terrorism, child pornography and so on but also about the reasons why a site comes up first or one company rather than another as a result of a search, that is to say, it is about the way the algorithms of service platforms work. In addition, the traceability of counterfeit and illegal products is taken into account.[37] What underlies the Commission's initiative is the principle that "what is forbidden in analogue must be forbidden online", in addition to the stated aim of wanting to take in hand the evolution of what has become the "normality" of our daily lives. All this is not left isolated in the economic and legal dimension but is included in an "Action Plan for Democracy": democracy should not only be supported but also defended against the distortions caused by the imposition of algorithms. Vice-President Vera Jourová announced

---

[37] As regards market distortions essentially due to so-called "gatekeepers", regulation is handed over to a Digital Market Act, which is intended to prevent rather than punish actions of abuse of a dominant position. A Data Governance Act is also planned (but in preparation).

this in early December 2020.

The last aspect, can be considered as the jewel in the crown: it is the new proposal for the regulation of artificial intelligence (AI) presented by the Commission in April 2021[38] to start the legislative process: the intention is not, of course, as has been repeatedly emphasised, to oppose the development of AI and its use, but to regulate those aspects that have an impact on the fundamental rights of citizens. Thus, the EC proposes to *ban* AI which produces "social scoring" (examining behaviours so as to prevent certain accesses), AI which manipulates human behaviour (through subliminal influences), AI which identifies people in real time through biometrics (except in exceptional and precisely indicated situations). Instead, the Commission intends to *regulate* AI involving a "high risk" with decisions that directly affect citizens' lives: for example, access to a loan, recruitment, dismissal, admission to university, entitlement to social benefits, but also border controls, asylum applications, autonomous driving of cars, and so on. It is true that the definition of "high risk" will give rise to discussions and differences, as will the assessment of conformity. Moreover, the acceptance or not of such a regulatory framework by international markets may lead to economic problems. In any event, the Commission also proposes the creation of a European AI Council, which could issue opinions, update the list of risks, or simply advise.

4.7   Conclusions

At this point, it seems that the time has come to conclude this examination of the challenges and potential opportunities which lie ahead for the European Union in the second half of the ninth parliamentary term: indeed, these are issues that will determine what the future of the Union will be for a long time to come. Before summarising the various topics discussed, however, I believe that attention should be

---

[38]You can find the document, the explanations and comments in https://ec.europa.eu/info/strategy/priorities-2019-2024/europe-fit-digital-age/excellence-trust-artificial-intelligence_en

drawn to two recent events which cannot merely be brushed aside as annoying incidents since they are likely to have a major influence on the future. The first one is the so-called "Sofagate" incident: it is in my opinion much more than an unpleasant event and a "protocol accident" caused by Turkey's President Erdogan during an official EU visit to that country and, from our point of view, even more than the gender inequality affront to a woman. It shows that there is something wrong at the institutional level in the EU: an unhealthy rivalry between the presidents of the two institutions, the Commission and European Council, which raises questions: is there a difference in rank? Are they equivalent? Is there a defined protocol? It is difficult to say. According to Turkey, in fact, the protocol solution adopted – which gave rise to the incident – was agreed upon by (someone in) Brussels. The second episode is one of governance: in August 2020, a European Commissioner, Phil Hogan, had to resign on the ground that he had not worn a mask and not respected social distancing (imposed by Covid) at a party of eighty people in his country (Ireland), without, moreover, placing himself in quarantine afterwards. Some analysts claimed that the new Irish government wanted to get rid of the Commissioner appointed by the previous government. That might be plausible, but, seen from the point of view of the EU, this is the first time that a European Commissioner has resigned under pressure from the government of his own country: this weakens the EU approach contains in the Code of conduct for Commissioners[39] where only the President of the European Commission can ask for resignation.

To conclude[40], it seems clear to me that the second half of the current legislature will be a decisive period, with the possibility of major work in prospect for the European Union. This is first because there is a Conference on the Future of Europe which will have to pro-

---

[39]The latest and most comprehensive version came into force on 1 February 2018. See EUR-Lex – 32018D0221(02) – EN – EUR-Lex (europa.eu)

[40]I am aware of the absence in this analysis od the dossier concerning environment and the related initiative known as Green Deal launched by the Commission as one of (or even "the") most important priorities: it is not a forgetfulness, it is because this topic deserves a specific treatment.

duce results: the words emerging by the open online debate, closely associated to the Union are *solidarity, unity and cooperation*, and for the future *hope and challenges*. Second, also because the ongoing battle to defend the founding values of the EU will leave its mark: the conflict on the importance and the conception of the founding values of the EU and liberal democracy, is becoming very serious and cannot be sidestepped during the Conference on the Future of Europe. Third, because there is historic action in the economy which is tending towards a structural change in European society: it must be clear that the funding responds to a strategic plan of the Union designed to change the European economy and society to make them more efficient, fairer and more sustainable. Forth, because the great achievement of free movement will have to be developed: that is essentially the strengthening of external borders and police cooperation with exchanges of information, with a view to eliminating all the internal border controls. And at the end, because the digital innovation progress is a big opportunity: we need to relaunch and strengthen European democracy also through the use of all the tools made available by digitalisation, digital democracy is an essential part of the strengthening of democracy *tout court*.

Chapter 5

Being Europeans in Times of Covid: Conclusions[*]

To entitle this chapter "Conclusions" is manifestly inappropriate because the issues it deals with are in a constant state of flux: along with them, the European Union itself is constantly in motion and has shown a good (if not excellent) degree of responsiveness. Consequently, there cannot be any genuine conclusions but only reflections: in any event – to recapitulate – the route traced by the four articles published here, written for CERIDAP, is made up of interweaving paths.

The first article appraises how, among its many effects, the Covid-19 health emergency has put the functioning of democratic institutions under unusual pressure: Parliaments are forced to give the executive branch powers to deal with the exceptional situation the virus has created. Without proper balancing measures, there are risks for democracy in the near future. The first article examines how the European Parliament has faced this challenge, both from a legal point of view and from that of the technological solutions which have been implemented, as a relevant example for future developments. The second article

---

*Unpublished, October 2021

takes up the same issue and goes deeper into it by considering the experience of the months that followed the first article, putting the emphasis on the role of the administration. In particular, the essential points of the reasoning developed in the second article concern the fact that Covid-19 has brought to the fore the role played by the administration as a bridge in the (conflictual) confrontation between the power of science and political power together with the fact that the health emergency has cast light on the importance of the functioning of parliamentary institutions for the defence of democracy because the executive branch (objectively) gets the upper hand. The administration of the European Parliament is a very interesting case study in this respect because it has succeeded in coping with the emergency thanks to several factors: working methods, digitisation and governance. The third article (the only one in Italian) considers what turned out to be the most tragic aspect of the pandemic along with the health aspect, namely the impact on work and its social consequences. The emergence of the pandemic has hit the labour market with the destruction of jobs and the failure to create new ones, while at the same time accentuating the disruptive processes under way (IT, mobility). The phenomenon is supranational and the European Union has been acting on two levels: facing up to the emergency (SURE, Youth initiative, EU Next Generation, etc.) and intervening on the basis of a strategy focused on investment in information technologies. It is these technologies which are changing how trades and professions are carried out, by reshaping the labour market while making it necessary for workers to upskill and have IT profiles and by creating a strong asymmetry between workers and their employment prospects. The last article takes stock midway through the ninth European legislature of the challenges facing Europe with an agenda made difficult by two years of health emergency: the challenges are huge, the projects and unfinished business under way are numerous and complex and all the European institutions are being called upon to cope with a situation which is admittedly delicate, yet pregnant with stimuli and potential. First of all, the Conference on the Future of Europe must be brought to a successful conclusion and, at the same time, there is the question of defending the founding values of the Union, in particular the rule of law and non-discrimination, which are the subject of disputes with some States[1]. Then there is the need to get the Next Generation EU operation – one of the most important political and economic initiatives in the continent's history – off on the right track. The next few years will also be decisive for assessing the validity and solidity of the agreement on Brexit and, at same time, for tackling the pressures on free movement brought about by emergencies. Lastly, there is the immense construction site of digitalisation with its various themes (artificial intelligence, Digital Service, teleworking, cybersecurity).

The fact is that, as I said above, these issues are in a perpetual state of flux.

In the current state of affairs it seems to me that during the pandemic emergency democracy in Europe has proved to be resilient and assertive. After the European Parliament, the national parliaments too have become aware of the importance of guaranteeing institutional balance in view also of the need to give more space to the executive: I think I can say that the authoritarian ambitions of the executive in the various Member States have been extremely restrained, also (but not only) thanks to the pressure exerted by the European Union, which has not missed an opportunity to denounce dangers and backsliding, as well as inspiring all its action and all its interventions during the Covid period by the founding values of democracy. I must say that on this point all three of the main European political institutions (Parliament, Council and Commission) have been in unison and the Member States have listened. In this context, the public administration, at all levels of government, has certainly played a decisive part in holding the system together. Of course, there are still open questions connected with the management of the pandemic. For example, everywhere in Europe the debate about whether vaccination should be made compulsory has been fraught with tension. But also (inde-

---

[1]When this book was already in its final drafts, news came in that the Polish Constitutional Court had declared that national law prevails over European law, thereby calling into question one of the main pillars of the European legal order: this development makes the battle to defend the rule of law, as a fundamental value of the EU, even more complicated. This will have to be followed up attentively.

pendently of the question of compulsory vaccination) there has been much discussion about the obligation to have a Green Pass in order to have access to certain activities (restaurants, theatres, concerts, etc.) and to the workplace, whether public or private. As usual, the explosion of organised violence (sometimes terrorist in nature) distorted a debate which could and should have been serious and serene, even when it was characterised by excessive recourse to the courts. In France, for example, a health minister (Agnès Buzyn) was put under investigation for her management of the pandemic crisis because she had allegedly "endangered the lives of others". Also in Belgium, for instance, hundreds of court cases were brought to have anti-Covid measures declared unlawful, so much so that the majority government launched an initiative for a framework law on the management of the pandemic, which was later abandoned. Meanwhile, in Italy, it fell to the Constitutional Court to declare (in September 2021) that it was constitutional for the President of the Council of Ministers to adopt urgent measures by decree to contain the pandemic. In any event, the European Commission also saw the need to establish a preliminary framework for reacting to health crises and proposed the creation of a European authority[2] to focus on crisis prevention.

The pandemic, it seems to me, has given an important impetus towards the creation of a true common economic system, in particular with the launch of Next Generation EU. The birth of a government of the European economy is a painful and resisted aspiration that has always been with us, starting with the original internal market and competition which gradually required the necessary steps forward to be taken: first policy coordination, then economic and social cohesion, hence convergence, so as to arrive at the common monetary policy. It was a long march to build the EMS, EMU and the Euro as instruments for governing the Community's economy. Moreover, the European management of the economic crisis generated in the USA in 2007-2008 and propagated for years was very effective (stability mechanism, aid and programming), despite the tense discussions on the rigour of national financial systems. Yet the feeling of incompleteness is still strong and centrifugal tendencies persist: the pandemic has finally

---

[2]HERA – Health Emergency Response Authority.

forced a more responsible reflection and for the first time in our history a European instrument has been created to guide and support growth, with investments and reforms, based on collective debt. It is certain that the results of this experiment will be decisive for the future of the Union. The pandemic has also given a boost to possible joint action in the area of employment, a sector jealously guarded by national governments: as we have seen, the EU's actions have been essential. Whereas as far as concerns the now central role of technology, the EU certainly did not wait for the pandemic to bring a strategic vision to bear on this[3].

In this context, the European Union is trying to reflect on the future by involving citizens: it is an important experiment, a great challenge which will have to be evaluated later on. Even the results of the Conference on the Future of Europe, once presented, will need time to produce their effects and to be properly assessed: there will certainly be no lack of analyses and no lack of criticism, which will be forthcoming whatever the outcome! As far as I am concerned, I believe that there are certain elements which constitute the necessary foundations for the construction of any European edifice for the future. These are elements that I have already highlighted over all these years, indeed decades, of direct European commitment in terms of action and reflection. First and foremost, on several occasions[4] I have emphasised what are the essential features of the Union: the Union has been built step by step, by discussions, negotiations and a common desire to move forward: it is not an imposition from above, made once and for all by an external actor; the Union is a democratic construction, since the European system is anchored in the principles and methods of democracy; its legal order is integrated with the national legal systems in a single, multilevel system of governance, it is not a parallel or juxtaposed system; the Union is constantly seeking to improve its functioning; the Union always works on the basis of jointly devised long-term strategies and uses the planning method ev-

---

[3]This aspect is largely and in depth analysed in G. Vilella, *E-Democracy. Dove ci porta la democrazia digitale*, Bologna, Pendragon, 2020.

[4]But essentially in G. Vilella, *Being European,* Nomos Verlag, Baden-Baden, 2017.

erywhere; as regards the economy, the Union is a system which seeks to reconcile the social aspect with productivity and competitiveness on the one hand, and growth with sustainability on the other; the Union is a completely open system which favours an active role for citizens, which it supports, protects and enriches with rights and powers; the Union is a system based on solid values which are ahead of the rest of the world.

The characteristics which I have just set forth must, in my view, continue to define the Union: only if we do not forget this starting point can we talk about the European Union in this 21st century, which opened with the Laeken European Council in December 2001 and the desire to build a more advanced and united Europe. Immediately afterwards, in March 2002, the Barcelona European Council envisaged a Europe with integrated economic development based on an inclusive social model of combating poverty. A few days earlier, on 28 February 2002, the solemn opening of the work of the Convention for a European Constitution took place, after it had been decided to start building the "greater" Europe with an enlargement of unprecedented dimensions. I wanted to recall these dates and passages in order not be omit from the analysis (as often occurs) the fact that our century began with a grandiose and exciting Europeanist project: those who scuttled this project bear a colossal historical responsibility. And yet the twenty years that followed and that we have lived through industriously have been very fruitful. In the meantime, the failure of the European Constitution nevertheless yielded the Lisbon Treaty, which, apart from marking a great advance in the process of European integration, also preserves the spirit of a constitution. All this was possible thanks to the intelligent adoption of the Berlin Declaration in March 2007, where the European Council succeeded in finding a compromise to unblock the situation and, at the same time, in relaunching the values of being together in the European Union. I have emphasised this factor too on several occasions[5], but I think it is useful to do so again in the situation in which we find ourselves. According to the Berlin Declaration, for a European: what is central is human beings (women and men), their inviolable dignity and

---

[5]But, also in this case, essentially in G. Vilella, *Being European, op. cit.*

their inalienable rights; there is a common goal: peace and freedom, democracy and the rule of law, mutual respect and responsibility, well-being and security, tolerance and participation, justice and solidarity; autonomy and the multiple traditions must be preserved, while open borders and the lively variety of languages, cultures and regions are to be regarded as enriching factors; the growing interdependence of the economy worldwide and the increasing competitiveness on international markets must be shaped according to our concepts and values; we must work to ensure that conflicts in the world are resolved peacefully and that people do not fall victim to war, terrorism or violence; we must promote freedom and development in the world, eradicate poverty, hunger and disease and play a leading role in this; in energy policy and climate protection we must play our part in preventing climate change; terrorism, organised crime and illegal immigration must be combated together and civil rights and freedoms must be defended also by standing up to their enemies; racism and xenophobia must no longer have a chance in Europe.

It seems obvious to me that we have now moved beyond the old paradigms of functionalism, federalism and the democratic deficit, which helped us to understand the phenomenon but which are now insufficient: it is now in the deep humus of the common European culture that the development and maturation of what are the deep values of Europe are being born, all together and not as alternatives. These are the values that, together with the characteristics listed above, must, in my opinion, continue to define the European Union of the future. The rest can be built on all this because, contrary to those who say that this is just mere rhetoric, these values are the structural foundations on which the Union's functioning mechanism can be installed. And there is much more to build. One important aspect, for example, is that it is certainly true that the European Parliament now occupies a central place, thereby consolidating the democratic nature of the Union (the European Parliament has made great strides with the Treaties of Maastricht, Amsterdam and Lisbon), yet it is still badly understood in communication and among citizens, with a large gap between its real powers and its popularity. The European Parliament has extensive legislative and important budgetary powers: in my opinion, the aspect that now needs to be developed more organically is the power to supervise the executive and the administration and hold them to account. The relationship between the European Parliament and the European Commission is crucial for determining the functioning of the politico-institutional system and fostering the creation of a European political space, which has long been an aspiration. Today we are witnessing real political debates between the various components, and for some time (since the eighth legislature) also attempts at real political alliances within the assembly. However, the national and governmental element constantly interrupts this kind of dialectic by introducing other criteria of judgement: but the national/governmental factor[6] is also an essential factor that cannot and must not be eliminated, because it is the expression of the Member States, the pillars of the Union. This shows the complexity of the system and the need to find a balance that cannot be based on a static model[7], in accordance with an unrealistic linearity: instead it is necessary constantly to seek out the positive factors which make for harmony. This means that in future – or better starting from now – we must give up the tendency, which has become more pronounced over the last few decades, to solve problems by differentiating, that is to say, by finding ad hoc solutions for those in favour of a particular action, leaving aside its opponents and further complicating the system by overlapping agreements and treaties.

The events of 2020-2021, the years of Covid and of the CERIDAP articles brought together in this volume, have nurtured and influenced the Union's evolutionary plan: the President of the Commission, Ursula von der Leyen, made this clear in her State of the Union ad-

---

[6]Of course, this has nothing to do with nationalism and sovereignism, which are inimical to the idea of a united Europe.

[7]For the meaning and consequences of the complexity of the Union system, see D. Innerarity, *Una teoria de la democracia compleja*, Galaxia Gutenberg, Barcelona ,2020, whilst for the difference between European democracy and traditional models, see M.J. Martinez Iglesias, *The Accidental Democracy: A European Model*, in S. Garben, I. Govaere and P. Nemitz (eds), *Critical Reflections on Constitutional Democracy in the European Union*, Hart Publishing, Oxford 2019.

dress[8] given in September 2021 before the European Parliament. To my mind, this is a very substantial speech which revolves around a fair and acute concept: the EU's reaction to the pandemic has shown that the Union has a soul and a sense of common responsibility, not only at the interinstitutional level but also at the intergovernmental level. In spite of a rather confused start by the Member States, it was around the Union that the right way to combat the pandemic was found, with major achievements ranging from Next Generation EU through the common digital certificate to permanent coordination in various areas. The Union has learned important lessons from this, which have led to the launch of new legislative projects, of which von der Leyen provided a circumstantial and reasoned list, without this weakening the two absolute priorities, which were and remain the climate and the defence of democracy as a founding value. This is not to forget that the events in connection with the withdrawal from Afghanistan have given new impetus to the idea of a common defence, to which von der Leyen devotes a great deal of space in her speech, which is as unusual as it is significant. This last element is an emblematic ornament to the rest of the evolutionary movement: "Europe will be forged in crises and will be the sum of the solutions adopted for those crises" Jean Monnet said, farsightedly, and the Covid pandemic is certainly a great *example* of this truth.

---

[8]State of the Union. Address 2021, by Ursula von der Leyen, https://ec.europa.eu/info/sites/default/files/soteu_2021_address_en_0.pdf.

References

(in the order as mentioned)

Y.N. HARARI, The world after coronavirus, Financial Times, 20 March 2020

Corriere della Sera, 25 March 2020

Bernard Demonty, Le Soir, 26 March 2020

IPU-Centre for Innovation in Parliament, Parliamentary Responses to Coronavirus, Live Document, March 2020

Decision of the President of the European Parliament, CP D(2020)9886, Brussels, 9 March 2020

Der Generalsekretär, Remote participation for Members in Parliamentary activities, D(2020)10901, 18 March 2020

TECHNICAL NOTES for the extraordinary meeting of the BUREAU on Friday 20 March 2020, Brussels, PE 649.203/BUR

DECISION OF THE BUREAU OF THE EUROPEAN PARLIAMENT of 20 March 2020 supplementing its Decision of 3 May 2004 on rules governing voting, PE 649.211/BU

Zeger VAN DER WAL, Being a Public Manager in Times of Crisis: The Art of Managing Stakeholders, Political Masters, and Collaborative Networks, in Public Administration Review, Vol. 80, Iss. 5, 2020

The Vocation Lectures (Edited and with an Introduction by D. OWEN and T.B. STRONG, Translation by R. LIVINGSTONE), Hackett, Indianapolis/Cambridge, 2004: Max WEBER, "Wissenschaft als Beruf" and "Politik als Beruf"

Massimo CACCIARI, Il lavoro dello spirito. Saggio su Max Weber, Adelphi, Milano, 2020

European Parliament resolution of 17 April 2020 on EU coordinated action to combat the COVID-19 pandemic and its consequences, P9_TA-PROV(2020)0054

POLITICO Brussels Playbook of 3 April 2020

European Parliament resolution of 17 December 2020, P9_TA-PROV(2020)03

G. VILELLA, Working methods of the European Parliament Administration in Multiactors World. A case-study, European Press Academic Publishing, Florence, 2019

G. VILELLA, The European Parliament Administration facing the challenge of eDemocracy, European Press Academic Publishing, Florence, 2021

G. VILELLA, E-Democracy. Dove ci porta la democrazia digitale, Pendragon, Bologna, 2020

Information and Communication Technology (ICT) in the European Parliament: Strategic orientations 2019-2021, authored by W. Petrucci, with the agreement of the Secretary General, D(2019)34304, October 2019

Gabriele BABINI, Logistics and Covid-19 pandemic. The European Parliament experience, PDF seminal presentation online, Brussels, 2 November 2020

Le comunicazioni del Presidente del Consiglio, Mario Draghi, al Senato della Repubblica sulle dichiarazioni programmatiche del Governo, Mercoledì, 17 Febbraio 2021, http://www.governo.it/it/articolo/le-comunicazioni-del-presidente-draghi-al-senato/16225

Monica Guerzoni, Corriere della Sera, 18 febbraio 2021

INPS, Osservatorio sul Precariato – Dati sui nuovi rapporti di lavoro, REPORT MENSILE GENNAIO – NOVEMBRE 2020, Roma, 10 febbraio 2021

Claudia Voltattorni, Corriere della Sera, 19 febbraio 2021

EPRS, Towards a more resilient Europe postcoronavirus. I: An initial mapping of structural risks facing the EU, PE 653.208, July 2021; II: Capabilities and gaps in the EU's capacity to dress structural risks, PE 652.024, October 2020: III: Options to enhance the EU's resilience to structural risks, PE 659.437, January 2021

https://ec.europa.eu/info/strategy/recovery-plan-europe_en

https://ec.europa.eu/regional_policy/en/funding/solidarity-fund/covid-19

https://ec.europa.eu/social/main.jsp?catId=1176

https://ec.europa.eu/social/main.jsp?catId=1036

https://ec.europa.eu/social/main.jsp?catId=101&langId=en1

ESPAS Report 2019: Global Trends to 2030, World Economic Forum 2020: COVID -19 Risks Outlook – A Preliminary Mapping and Its Implications, 2020, OECD Employment Outlook 2019: The Future of Work, 2019, and Eurofound: Living, working and COVID-19 – First findings – April 2020

COM(2010)245 final, Bruxelles, 19.5.2010

COM(2015)192 final, Bruxelles, 6.5.2015

COM(2020)67 final, Bruxelles, 19.2.2020

Marco Galluzzo, Corriere della Sera, 15 febbraio 2021

Opening Statement in the European Parliament Plenary Session by Ursula von der Leyen, Candidate for President of the European Commission (europa.eu)

European Parliament resolution of 15 January 2020 on the position of the European Parliament on the Conference on the Future of Europe, P9_TA(2020)0010

https://www.europarl.europa.eu/doceo/document/TA-9-2020-0010_EN.html

Communication from the Commission to the European Parliament and the Council, Shaping the Conference on the Future of Europe, 22.1.2020, COM(2020) 27 final

https://eur-lex.europa.eu/legalcontent/EN/TXT/?uri=CELEX%3A52020DC0027

European Parliament resolution of 18 June 2020 on the European Parliament's position on the Conference on the Future of Europe, P9 TA(2020)015

https://www.europarl.europa.eu/doceo/document/TA-9-2020-0153_EN.html

Presidency of the Council of the European Union, Conference on the Future of Europe, AG32 INST120, Brussels, 24 June 2020, setting out in detail the Council position as agreed at the Permanent Representative Committee, https://www.consilium.europa.eu/media/44679/st09102-en20.pdf 7POLITICO Brussels Playbook, 30 July 2021, https://www.politico.eu/newsletter/brussels-playbo

ok/politico-brussels-playbook-time-to-say-goodbye-no-eulogies-th ough-over-and-out/

2020 Rule of law report – Communication and country chapters

https://ec.europa.eu/info/publications/2020-rule-law-report-comm unication-and-country-chapters_en

Le Soir, 14-15 August 2018

Regulation (EU, Euratom) 2020/2092 of the European Parliament and of the Council of 16 December 2020 on a general regime of conditionality for the protection of the Union budget, OJ L 433I, 22.12.2020

Case C-156/21 Hungary v. European Parliament and Council, OJ C 138, 19.4.2021

Case C-157/21 Poland v. European Parliament and Council, OJ 138, 19.4.2021

Diana-Urania GALETTA, Karlsruhe über alles? The reasoning on the principle of proportionality in the judgment of 5 May 2020 of the German BVerfG and its consequences, CERIDAP, 2/2020

Jacques ZILLER, The unbearable heaviness of the German consti- tutional judge. On the judgment of the Second Chamber of the German Federal Constitutional Court of 5 May 2020 concerning the European Central Bank, CERIDAP, 4/2020

European Commission, Statement by European Commission Presi- dent on the new Hungarian bill that discriminates against people based on their sexual orientation, Brussels, 23 June 2021, https:// ec.europa.eu/commission/presscorner/detail/en/STATEMENT_2 1_3164

Euronews, 23 June 2021, https://www.euronews.com/2021/06/23/hu ngary-s-anti-lgbt-law-is-a-shame-says-ursula-von-der-leyen

Notre mode de vie est le meilleur bouclier contre les d'érives, Le Soir, 30 June 2021

https://cdn.g4media.ro/wp-content/uploads/2021/06/Sassoli-Letter -EC-230621.pdf

Resolution of 17 December 2020, P9_TA(2020)0360; Resolution of 25 March 2021, P9_TA(2021)0103

Resolution of 10 June 2021, P9_TA(2021)0287

https://ec.europa.eu/commission/presscorner/detail/en/ip_21_342 4

European Recovery Plan, https://ec.europa.eu/info/live-work-travel -eu/health/coronavirus-response/recovery-plan-europe_it

R (on the application of Miller) v. Prime Minister [2019] UKSC 41

Jacques ZILLER, Brexit: to have or not to have a deal? (first episode) – The New Brexit Deal: Predictable Outcome of a Lose-Lose Negotiation. A First Glance Assessment of the EU-UK Trade Agreement 24.12.2020 (second episode) CERIDAP, 4/2020

Valerio Onida, Corriere della Sera, 29 August 2019

Sabino Cassese, Corriere della Sera, 22 August 2017

Exploring Digital Government Transformation in the EU – Understanding public sector innovation in a data-driven society, Misuraca, G., Barcevičius, E. and Codagnone, C. editor(s), EUR 30333 EN, Publications Office of the European Union, Luxembourg, 2020

https://ec.europa.eu/info/strategy/priorities-2019-2024/europe-fit -digital-age/excellence-trust-artificial-intelligence_en

EUR-Lex – 32018D0221(02) – EN – EUR-Lex (europa.eu)

G. VILELLA, Being European, Nomos Verlag, Baden Baden, 2017

D. INNERARITY, Una teoria de la democracia compleja, Galaxia Gutenberg, Barcelona ,2020

M.J. MARTINEZ IGLESIAS, The Accidental Democracy: A European Model, in S. Garben, I. Govaere and P. Nemitz (eds), Critical Reflections on Constitutional Democracy in the European Union, Hart Publishing, Oxford 2019

State of the Union. Address 2021, by Ursula von der Leyen, https:// ec.europa.eu/info/sites/default/files/soteu_2021_address_en_0 .pdf

Photo Credits

www.ingramcontent.com/pod-product-compliance
Lightning Source LLC
Chambersburg PA
CBHW051446150726
48000CB00005B/2281